ELOGOS

Daily Devotions for Down-To-Earth Disciples
2

Deb Grant

i

ELOGOS

DAILY DEVOTIONS FOR DOWN-TO-EARTH DISCIPLES
2

BY DEB GRANT

Scripture quotations from *New Revised Standard Version of the Bible* @ 1989 by the National Council of Churches of Christ in the USA. All rights reserved: used by permission.

Cover design: Debra Grant
Front cover photo: Megan Purser
About the cover photo: Ryan Purser on coast of Ireland
Author Photo: Kris Siegert Pool
Echo Lake Photography

ISBN: 978-0-9824226-1-8

To
My Goddaughter
Kacy Shea

Acknowledgements

Writing ELOGOS has been a daily discipline for me for more than 15 years. I have very little in my life that I have done consistently over that long a time. I have plenty of stupid little habits and only a few truly good ones. ELOGOS is one of my better habits. I believe the Word of God coaxes amazing things from us. ELOGOS is my honest and best attempt at following Jesus in my own flawed manner for the sake of others.

I am deeply grateful to my friends who encouraged my writing. Heath & Erica Abel are friends who have often championed my gifts and nagged me to keep writing. It is a joy when we bring out the best in one another.

I cherish all the subscribers to the ELOGOS devotions email list who daily attend to God's Word through the discipline of reading ELOGOS. They represent hundreds of vocations and relationships. They serve God in often quiet ways. They allow me the privilege of walking with them in their lives of faith and my own faith is strengthened because of them.

I am grateful to Cats Sonnenburg for volunteering to help proof read my drafts and to Jessica Raphael for editorial assistance.

I pray that my goddaughter, Kacy Shea, will continue to enjoy the God who loves, chases and splashes her life with grace and purpose now and always.

Deb Grant

Introduction

ELOGOS first took the form of devotions emailed to students at Texas A&M University in College Station where I served as a campus pastor. The word 'logos' in Greek means 'Word' and more specifically, God's Word. The 'E' first stood for email. For this book, 'E' stand for 'everyday.' ELOGOS 2 is a second year of daily devotions.

For a generation who is accustomed to the shortness of text messages, I have intentionally kept the messages brief, but I hope that they have a long lasting effect. Most of the scripture selections were chosen on the basis of the text suggested by the New Revised Common Lectionary. I wrote each meditation on a word or phrase that rose to the surface as I read them each morning. I consider myself a "pedestrian theologian" – one whose faith is a journey alive in God's Word and alive in the down-to-earth experiences of daily life.

I pray that these bits of scripture, my humble words and earnest prayers will be a blessing to you wherever you are on your journey of faith.

Deb Grant

January 1

Genesis 1:14-15
And God said, "Let there be lights in the dome of the sky to separate the day from the night; and let them be for signs and for seasons and for days and years, and let them be lights in the dome of the sky to give light upon the earth." And it was so.

■ ■ ■

From the beginning, God has taught us to measure our days. There is a great grace in the beginning of a new year. We long to slough our old habits and attitudes off like a snake sheds its skin. Snakes shed their eye caps off too. Everything that has become worn or diseased or dull slips away. If only troubles were so easily tossed to the side of the road. If only our limited sight could be so quickly granted clarity. God shines his light on us and the first thing we can see is our need for wholeness, forgiveness, and mercy. The calendar flips to a new year and sparks our longing to begin our lives anew. With each rising of the sun, each passing of an old year into a new one, we are offered reminders of Christ's Easter gift for us all....a new life. It begins today and again tomorrow. The gift of God's Easter was born at Christmas so that every day and every year of our lives now and forever will be a brand new adventure.

■ ■ ■

Holy God, bless this new year with your presence and this new day with our whole hearts alive with you. Amen.

1

January 2

Hebrews 1:2
But in these last days he has spoken to us by a Son, whom
he appointed heir of all things, through whom he also
created the worlds.

■ ■ ■

I have a little friend named Elli whose entry into the world
and growth ever since I have had the privilege of
witnessing. She has grown in her ability to express herself.
Elli was capable in infancy of blood-chilling screams that
could make drywall crumble. She moved to more complex
vocabulary that helped her acquire a taste of some favorite
food like "Guacamole" to the flawless recitation of one of the
household rules "No excessive whining." The first sounds of
Jesus, the Savior of the world, were the sounds of a baby's
cry. He grew to become a man whose words would rock the
world. His words were simple and yet they called humanity
to look at life and others differently. The baby we celebrated
at Christmas would grow into the one whose name would be
the source of grace and truth. We enjoy the baby talk and
the efforts of children shaping new words. The noise of an
infant born to be a savior became the first sounds of hope.

■ ■ ■

Gentle Jesus, you grew up and learned to say the words we
need to hear. Amen.

January 3

Matthew 3:17
And a voice from heaven said, "This is my Son, the Beloved, with whom I am well pleased."

■ ■ ■

As a child, I attended a father-daughter dinner with my Dad. During the dinner, each person was invited to stand and introduce themselves. One by one a man and a girl rose to their feet and then the man introduced himself by his own name and then his daughter. My Dad had been injured as a teenager in an auto accident and his leg had never healed properly. It made standing gracefully difficult. He would often use our shoulder as a crutch. The feel of the pressure of his huge hand on me was always more of an honor than a burden but he would move his hand away quickly. This time when he stood, he didn't remove his hand and when he spoke he introduced me first. He said, "This is Deb Grant and I am her Dad, Cal." I felt a thousand feet tall. The power of our baptism in recalling it every day is in the fact that God names us his sons and daughters who are loved and needed in the kingdom of God. Who are we to argue with that? Who would want to?

■ ■ ■

Lord God, you know us by our name and we are yours indeed. Amen.

3

January 4

Isaiah 49:4
But I said, "I have labored in vain, I have spent my
strength for nothing and vanity; yet surely my cause is with
the Lord, and my reward with my God."

■ ■ ■

We all want to see that our work makes a difference, that our existence matters. Politicians invented the art of spin doctoring to turn difficult situations into positive ones. Unfortunately, we have to do some major spin doctoring in our thinking to believe that our day-to-day chores amount to much of anything. Thinking that our daily work brings glory to God is a stretch on average days. My work is often flawed or inadequate, yet there is certain nobility, if not outrageous confidence, in offering to God our most mundane chores and fractured gifts. It is a statement of faith and hope that God can use as the foundation of the future. Don't ask me how God does that. There are plenty of days I don't know why God does that, but time after time....God takes what we have to offer, however ordinary and unshaped and makes it good.

■ ■ ■

Lord God, receive the meditations of our hearts and the works of our hands as a gift to you who loves us so well. Amen.

January 5

Psalm 40:1,3
I waited patiently upon the Lord; he stooped to me and
heard my cry. He put a new song in my mouth, a song of
praise to our God; many shall see, and stand in awe, and
put their trust in the Lord.

■　■　■

I can safely say that I have waited upon the Lord but I can't
say I've always waited patiently. That impatience makes
itself known in speaking before I had anything worthwhile
to say, acting before I had anything to give without strings
attached, or plodding forward before talking or listening to
God. The outcomes of those impatient acts were everything
from sloppy missteps to hurtful events. To that mess, God
still chooses to come. Through his word, God lifts us up,
dusts us off, ties our dangling shoe laces, and gives us a
view from a higher place. God has done that for generations
and God does that for us. When we consider how many
times in our lives God has entered into our messes, we
experience a trust that surfaces more quickly. And just as
quickly, we remember how to sing.

■　■　■

Help us, Lord, to remember how patient you are with us.
Amen.

January 6

I Corinthians 1:8-9
He will also strengthen you to the end, so that you may be
blameless on the day of our Lord Jesus Christ. God is
faithful; by him you were called into the fellowship of his
Son, Jesus Christ our Lord.

■ ■ ■

God's grace will save us. Justify us, like the words on this
page are justified to look even on both sides of the
paragraph. God's grace makes us right. God does and will
wipe our noses, straighten our collars, take the smudge off
our faces. God will take the life of his own Son for our
miserable failures. God never stops believing that we are
worth saving. As big and as magnificent and relentless as
that grace of God is, I still have trouble believing it myself.
Grace still has trouble sinking into my sorry soul. That we
could walk into ANY day much less the Lord's Day as
blameless reels my imagination. We continue to be called
into being in the company of Christ not because we are
worthy but because we have been made worthy by the grace
of God. I don't always understand that....but I always need
it.

■ ■ ■

Holy God, your invitation to join you in your mission is an
overwhelming statement of your grace. Amen.

January 7

John 1:37-38
The two disciples heard him say this and they followed
Jesus. When Jesus turned and saw them following, he said
to them, "What are you looking for?" They said to him,
"Rabbi, where are you staying?" He said to them, "Come
and see."

■ ■ ■

"What are you looking for?" Ask any one of us that question on any given day and we will either have an answer on the tip of our tongue or we will ponder it. We will ponder it because there are so many things we are looking for. We will rarely ever say "Who me? I am not looking for anything!" We are all looking for something. Clarity. Peace. Strength. Happiness. A friend. Freedom. Justice. Hope. Love. Forgiveness. Meaningful work. Understanding. Health. A good night's sleep. Peace inside our own skin. The idea that any one person could be the key to all of that is laughable. Those who expect it all from one human being fail in their attempts and often shatter any hope of a relationship. There is one person who is willing to take it all on and can handle the pressure. Jesus invites us to come and see.

■ ■ ■

You invite us, Lord, to come and see who you can be in our lives. Give us the courage to accept. Amen.

January 8

Isaiah 9:2,4
The people who walked in darkness have seen a great light;
those who lived in a land of deep darkness - on them light
has shined. For the yoke of their burden, and the bar across
their shoulders, the rod of their oppressor, you have broken
as on the day of Midian.

■ ■ ■

It's the old adage - the bad times help us appreciate the
good times; the darkness - the light, etc. This logic leads us
to the old joke about what the guy who was hitting himself
in the head with a hammer said when asked why he was
doing it - "Because it feels so good when I stop." The
difference between the happiness that we can create
ourselves artificially and the joy that God gives to us is that
God's joy can be seen in the darkness, felt with the burdens,
known inside hunger. Our happiness is a fleeting moment
like passing through the path of the sun on a cold day. It is
good. We revel in the moment of such happiness. God's joy
is a promise that burns like a furnace that fuels our hope,
our homes, and our souls even as we walk in darkness and
feel the yoke of our burdens.

■ ■ ■

Grant us joy, O Lord, so that it can warm us through our
cold days. Amen.

January 9

Psalm 27:8-9
'Come,' my heart says, 'seek his face!' Your face, Lord, do I
seek. Do not hide your face from me. Do not turn your
servant away in anger, you who have been my help. Do not
cast me off, do not forsake me, O God of my salvation!

■ ■ ■

I was reading an article about communication, particularly in academic and corporate settings. The aspect of communication we most ignore and teach the least is how to listen. We certainly bark at one another and say, "Will you please listen!" or "Listen up, people!" but careful listening is a discipline that needs to be learned and practiced. Listening is one of the more often forgotten aspects of prayer. We learn how to talk to God but have trouble knowing what it means to listen to God. When we have trouble hearing one another, we incline our ear in the direction of the voice. We are used to sounds coming at us from the outside in, but God speaks to us from the inside out and so it may be just a matter of learning to listen in God's direction. We are just so often surprised that God's voice could be heard inside our own hearts.

■ ■ ■

Teach me how to listen in your direction, Lord. Amen.

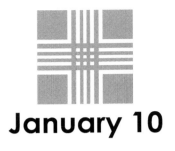

January 10

I Corinthians 1:10-11
Now I appeal to you, brothers and sisters, by the name of
our Lord Jesus Christ, that all of you be in agreement and
that there be no divisions among you, but that you be
united in the same mind and the same purpose. For it has
been reported to me by Chloe's people that there are
quarrels among you, my brothers and sisters.

■ ■ ■

Paul appeals for unity and yet, he knows they are fighting among themselves. Almost in the same breath, he calls them brothers and sisters twice. And the real kicker is that Paul isn't talking about Christians vs. Non-Christians. He is talking about internal strife inside the Christian community. There are still too many who believe that church people are supposed to get along perfectly. It doesn't matter that these words were written centuries ago. The Body of Christ continues to need to hear the chastisement. We will always have differences but the cross unites us. The powers at work in the world follow the laws of physics – it takes energy to stay together. Our natural inclination is to be apart. As Christians in community, our differences don't magically disappear, but the power of Christ gives us the ability to defy the physics that would drive us apart.

■ ■ ■

Bind us together, Lord, that we might be one in you. Amen.

January 11

Matthew 4:21-22
As he went from there, he saw two other brothers, James
son of Zebedee and his brother John, in the boat with their
father Zebedee, mending their nets, and he called them.
Immediately they left the boat and their father, and
followed him.

■   ■   ■

Though I know the emphasis in this passage is the calling
of the disciples, my heart can't help but feel for Zebedee left
in the boat to mend his nets without his sons. Who knows -
perhaps they were messing up the nets anyway - perhaps
they were driving Zeb crazy. Those two would become
known as the "sons of thunder" so Zeb might have
welcomed the peace and quiet. Or perhaps he did not want
them to leave but was just as compelled by Jesus. Though
he could not leave to follow Jesus himself, Zebedee could
offer him the most precious thing he could - his sons. So
compelled by the need of the world for a savior, God did the
same thing for us - offered us his son.

■   ■   ■

Holy God, may we offer you the best of who are. Amen.

January 12

Micah 6:8
He has told you, O mortal, what is good; and what does the
Lord require of you but to do justice, and to love kindness,
and to walk humbly with your God?

■ ■ ■

The first step in growing a relationship with God is recognizing that God is God and we are not. Given who God is, it makes sense to ask what the Lord requires of us. We understand what it means to be under someone in authority who has expectations of us. When human beings are in authority, at our best, we demand good work and behavior and at our worst, we demand more than we deserve. God's expectations of us are surprisingly basic. God wants us to treat one another well, and to treat him with awe and respect. Human beings have not had a great history of living up to God's expectations. Jesus came to show us how it could be done and to give us the grace we needed to keep trying. By dying again in Christ and rising again to new life, we grow in our relationship with God by having a passion for justice, kindness and humility.

■ ■ ■

You, O Lord, are worthy of honor. Teach us to love like you. Amen.

January 13

Luke 3:22
And a voice came from heaven, "You are my Son, the
Beloved; with you I am well pleased."

■ ■ ■

We are a critical people. Our criticism of one another is
often pointed and specific with little wiggle room for
argument. Our compliments are often more general and
consequently, easier to dismiss as idle flattery. The power
of a well-timed, specific compliment is not to be underestimated. It can put a person who has stumbled on their
feet again. God's words to his Son Jesus were not empty
flattery, but a declaration of who he was, to whom he
belonged and how God felt about him. There was no other
option than to accept or reject it. We tend to be a people
who are more ready to accept God's judgment of us than we
are to accept God's declaration that we belong to God and
that God is pleased with us.

■ ■ ■

Today, Lord, we claim our baptismal birthright of being
your child - forgiven, redeemed and loved. Amen.

January 14

I Corinthians 1:26-27,29
Consider your own call, brothers and sisters: not many of
you were wise by human standards, not many were
powerful, not many were of noble birth. But God chose what
is foolish in the world to shame the wise; God chose what is
weak in the world to shame the strong....so that no one
might boast in the presence of God.

■　■　■

I have a colleague who reads, listens to music, and watches movies regularly. He absorbs wisdom and integrates that wisdom into his sermons, writings, and his conversations. I have a friend who remembers and reflects intelligently on the most amazing details from novels and, historical and current events. I itch to be like them. I envy their intellect and ability to take in and share knowledge. Their greatest source of wisdom, however, is not the inner workings of the synapses of their brains. It is not their keen minds and cognitive abilities, but their overwhelming compassion. In the presence of the Lord and in the shadow of the cross, we are confronted with a new kind of wisdom that the world cannot readily explain or live well without. It is love.

■　■　■

God of Love, grant us the wisdom of a smart heart. Amen.

January 15

Matthew 5:3,5
Blessed are the poor in spirit, for theirs is the kingdom of heaven. Blessed are the meek, for they will inherit the earth.

■　■　■

I know what it is like to be poor in spirit. I have known down days and heavy weeks. I don't do meek much. I swing between blustering bravado and self-depreciated moroseness. Neither are very pretty. Neither are anywhere near the gentle posture of those who I would describe as meek. Meek doesn't mean letting oneself be used as a doormat, but it does mean moving through the world with fewer defenses and less energy for retaliation. To be invulnerable is to be unapproachable and cold. To be completely vulnerable is to spend our days experiencing the agony of being a victim. Somewhere in the midst of all that chaos are the meek ones. To be blissfully meek is to know when to open a window and when to shut a door. It isn't any wonder to me why they are blessed with inheriting the earth. We are blessed to stand in their presence and learn from them.

■　■　■

Lord God, may we learn from one another how to live in peace. Amen.

January 16

Exodus 24:12-13
The LORD said to Moses, "Come up to me on the mountain,
and wait there; and I will give you the tablets of stone, with
the law and the commandment, which I have written for
their instruction." So Moses set out with his assistant
Joshua, and Moses went up into the mountain of God.

■ ■ ■

As often as I have read or heard this passage, I never noticed Joshua. This is a story about God and Moses. The tale is overwhelmed with God and Moses, a mountain and commandments. Joshua the assistant that Moses brought with him obviously did not call much attention to himself. Joshua might have been a young man, perhaps even a boy. Nevertheless, Joshua served with loyalty at Moses' side. When the time was right, Joshua became the central person in the story. Joshua led God's people where Moses could not go into the promised land. There is something to be said for those who learn and grow, serve with loyalty and respond to God's call. They rarely call a great deal of attention to themselves, but the future of the Kingdom of God rests on their shoulders. If we look around us today, we will see them. They are listening to us and learning from our faith. What will they learn from us today?

■ ■ ■

Holy God, bless those who listen from the wings for their part in the great story. Amen.

January 17

Isaiah 42:3
A bruised reed he will not break, and a dimly burning wick
he will not quench; he will faithfully bring forth justice.

■ ■ ■

The kind of leadership that Christ embodied stood in contrast to the models of leaders throughout history. We have known those who rule by physical force, military dominance, terror, and political manipulation. For those leaders, it serves them well when they can feed on human fear or greed. The rule of Christ, though awesome in power, was characterized by gentleness. He did not reduce people to quivering masses who would jump at the protection he offered or surface their basest addictions. The scriptures are filled with story after story of individual encounters with Jesus. He met people where they were. He accepted people in their sinfulness and need and then, invited them to a new way of life. Quietly and tenderly, Christ changed the lives of people - one person at a time. Jesus made disciples one disciple at a time. It wasn't the fastest way to change the world, but it worked. It still does. One disciple at a time.

■ ■ ■

Holy God, teach us that there is power in leading with compassion. Amen.

17

January 18

Psalm 29:8,11
The voice of the Lord makes the oak trees writhe and strips
the forest bare....The Lord shall give strength to his people;
the Lord shall give his people the blessing of peace.

■ ■ ■

It is interesting to me that the Lord has the power to make
trees shiver with his voice and peace to his people. Usually
voices with that much power only cause us to quake inside
our shoes. Power and peace as human inventions are
constantly at odds with one another. Peace might result
from a power display of force but the kind of peace that
results is not an easy one. We know how to be powerful but
we don't always know how to make for peace. We know
peace when we experience it but we are often too powerless
to make it happen for ourselves much less our neighbor.
Inside the mystery of God's character, however, such
contradictions don't exist. Perhaps the peace God offers us
is resting in the knowledge that we can't always be big and
strong. We can't always get it right. We can't always be
what everyone expects us to be. Peace is knowing that even
and especially in the face of our in-adequacy and
powerlessness, we are God's.

■ ■ ■

Take our lives, Lord, in your powerful presence and grant
us the peace to be your strong people. Amen.

January 19

Acts 19:1
While Apollo was in Corinth, Paul passed through the
interior regions and came to Ephesus, where he found some
disciples. He said to them, "Did you receive the Holy Spirit
when you became believers?" They replied, "No, we have
not even heard that there is a Holy Spirit."

■ ■ ■

Church membership is declining. People are rejecting religious institutional organizations to live their spirituality more individually. The Church is slowly getting a clue that it cannot be an exclusive club. We have made the Christian faith an obstacle course of hoops to jump through rather than an authentic journey of relationship. Even during the first centuries when the disciples were taking their baby steps, there was a need and a purpose for community. We need one another. We may not need the budget, the politics and the hoop-jumping of our club-like Christian churches but we still need the Body of Christ. Discipleship is a team sport not a personal hobby. John the Baptist's ministry created disciples for Jesus Christ. Their discipleship needed the nurture of the other Christians like Paul to deepen their knowledge and faith. So do we.

■ ■ ■

Lord, help us to admit what we don't know, fearlessly seek out those on the journey with us, and help us to offer unselfishly who we are in Christ. Amen.

January 20

Mark 1: 10-11
And just as he was coming up out of the water, he saw the
heavens torn apart and the Spirit descending like a dove on
him. And a voice came from heaven, "You are my Son, the
Beloved; with you I am well pleased. "

■ ■ ■

When my father wanted to get our attention, he yelled. But
he had a much deeper impact on me when he said the
words, "I am disappointed in you." I can't imagine what
those words, "my son, beloved, well pleased" meant to
Jesus. I know in my soul what they would mean for me to
hear from God. Jesus' ministry began when he stepped out
of his own baptismal waters. His mission that began in that
moment was in part to make sure that you and I would
hear that we belong to God, that we are greatly loved and
that we are not a disappointment.

■ ■ ■

Lord God, we are your children and we long to hear your
voice, know your love and believe your affirmation. Amen.

January 21

I Samuel 3:8,10
The Lord called Samuel again, a third time. And he got up
and went to Eli, and said, "Here I am, for you called me."
Then Eli perceived that the Lord was calling the boy. So
Samuel went and lay down in his place. Now the Lord came
and stood there, calling as before, "Samuel! Samuel!" And
Samuel said, "Speak, for your servant is listening."

■ ■ ■

I have a friend who calls me often while he is driving. The cell phone connection will sometimes be lost. If we are in the midst of telling a story and get disconnected, it may be several minutes before we figure out that no one is listening. When we get reconnected we have to ask, "What was the last thing you heard?" The answer to that question might be rather embarrassing since we might have talked a long time into an empty phone. Our relationship with the Lord involves listening as much as it involves speaking. God's Word provides his voice. Sometimes that word comes pulled through the faith lives of those around us. Sometimes, we need to have people like Eli, to remind us to pay attention. The Lord's voice is truly present for those who let him get a word in edgewise.

■ ■ ■

Lord, speak...for your servant is listening. Amen.

21

January 22

Psalm 139:1-2
O Lord, you have searched me and known me. You know
when I sit down and when I rise up; you discern my
thoughts from far away. You search out my path and my
lying down, and are acquainted with all my ways.

■ ■ ■

Living alone, I have the luxury of not having to explain my
personal habits to anyone or force anyone to step over my
messes or hold me accountable to household chores. At the
same time, I am not as skilled as those who must adjust,
adapt, be attentive to and negotiate with those with whom
they live. Neither do I experience daily what it means to
have people who know me so well that emotions and
gestures can be read. It does happen occasionally and it is,
at once, unnerving and filled with a lesson in how love is
supposed to work. Love works with wisdom and grace and
not a little laughter. We may be tempted to hide from the
presence of the Lord who knows us so well and yet, we
know there is freedom and joy in being so well known.

■ ■ ■

Lord God, may we learn from you the joy and wonder of
being attentive to those around us. In the name of Jesus,
Amen.

January 23

I Corinthians 6:12, 20
"All things are lawful for me," but not all things are
beneficial. "All things are lawful for me, " but I will not be
dominated by anything......do you not know that your body
is a temple of the Holy Spirit within you, which you have
from God, and that you are not your own? For you were
bought with a price; therefore glorify God in your body.

■ ■ ■

We are saved by grace through faith in Christ. Minding our
manners, giving to charity, keeping our nose out of other
people's business, being moral in the use of alcohol and
sexual expression will make us better human beings and at
peace inside our own skin. Those acts will not make us
Christian or better than anyone else. As Christians, we
have the freedom to choose to give some of our freedom
away so that God is honored by what we do and so that
others will be treated with dignity and respect. We are
obedient to the law not because we are afraid....but because
we are free.

■ ■ ■

Precious Lord, help us this day to exercise our freedom to be
obedient to your law of love. Amen.

January 24

John 1:45-46
Philip found Nathanael and said to him, "We have found him about whom Moses in the law and also the prophets wrote, Jesus son of Joseph from Nazareth." Nathanael said to him, "Can anything good come out of Nazareth?" Philip said to him, "Come and see."

■ ■ ■

Being unabashedly Lutheran, I understand our revulsion of the strong-armed tactics of well-meaning Christians to evangelize. At the same time, I am no less compelled to share the good news of God in Jesus Christ. One person once defined evangelism as one beggar telling another beggar where to find bread. I love the sublime beauty of Philip's invitation - "Come and see." He does not ask Nathanael to check his brains at the door. He simply invites him to see for himself who Jesus is. The Holy Spirit convicts and converts. We can only speak of what we have seen and heard. Jesus changed the world. He loves and forgives me. He keeps me from being so full of myself that I am no earthly good. If you have questions, doubts, or a pit in your stomach hungry for bread - "Come and see."

■ ■ ■

Lord God, pull your good news through me to others so that others may know your freedom and your love. Amen.

January 25

Mark 9:42
If any of you put a stumbling block before one of these little ones who believe in me, it would be better for you if a great millstone were hung around your neck and you were thrown into the sea.

■　■　■

Driven by a sweet tooth, I broke the commandment about not stealing at an early age. I would steal candy bars from a local market near my school. My career as a thief didn't last much more than a week but long enough to have taught a classmate some of my thieving techniques. I felt guilty enough for the crime, but as the years went along I felt even more guilty about enticing someone else to sin. I have known my share of stumbling blocks in my journey of faith. I learned early, however, that I could be a stumbling block as easily as I could have one. One of the great wonders of God's economy is that the more we resist hurting others, the more strength we will have to overcome the obstacles thrown our way. If we concentrate only on walking the straight and narrow ourselves, we may miss the opportunity to help someone over their difficulties. To lose ourselves in order to find ourselves may not make much sense but it is a powerful way to love.

■　■　■

Lord God, forgive our self-absorbed focus and help us find ourselves in loving others. Amen.

January 26

Jonah 3:1-2
The word of the Lord came to Jonah a second time, saying,
"Get up, go to Nineveh, that great city, and proclaim to it
the message that I tell you. "

■ ■ ■

When the word of the Lord came to Jonah the first time, he peeled off in another direction and found himself drenched in whale spit. The story of Jonah is laced with grace. Grace abounds in the simple phrase, "the Lord came to Jonah a second time." We live in an age of cultural attention-deficit. If something or someone doesn't work or feel right or offends us, we move on. We change the channel. We surf elsewhere. We give up. We give up on one another at the same time knowing how awful it feels to be the one on which others give up. God could have given up on Jonah - he had plenty of reasons. But God came to Jonah a second time. We are all children of God's second times.

■ ■ ■

Holy God, we give you thanks for your grace and ask that you give us the wisdom and the will to extend it to others. Amen.

January 27

Psalm 62:6-7
He alone is my rock and my salvation, my fortress; I shall
not be shaken. On God rests my deliverance and my honor;
my mighty rock, my refuge is in God.

■ ■ ■

It is a windy day today. We have a tendency to underestimate the power of wind. I remember deciding to walk on a beach once on a particularly windy day. I thought, "How bad can it be? It is always windy at the beach." But the gale blew sideways and pummeled my face with sand. I have seen wind stir oceans and toss giant ships. Our lives tend to have "windy days" in which stuff gets thrown in our face. We are buffeted by the words and needs of others and normal activities seem that much harder to do. We look for barriers against the wind, but in the end we need a solid, quiet place away from the opinions and demands to hear our own soul's voice and rest on God's most solid grace.

■ ■ ■

Our souls wait in silence, Lord, for the hope we know is in you. Amen.

January 28

I Corinthians 7:31
And those who deal with the world as though they had no
dealings with it. For the present form of this world is
passing away.

■ ■ ■

Since the time of the resurrection of Christ, many different
theological ideas have developed about where life as we
know it is headed. The ideas mirror our own mental and
emotional state. There are pessimists and optimists. Some
say the world is getting worse and worse and everything
and everyone is going to "hell in a hand basket." They say
the best we can do is keep our noses clean and duck. Some
say the world is getting better and better and we must be
vigilant warriors for stomping out sin. Some of these folks
haven't figured out how to leave the sinner intact while
doing all that stomping. Both say the time will come when
the world as we know it will end. Christ shall reign
completely. Getting ready for it means not holding on so
tightly to the things we will let go of quickly to grab our
Savior's hand.

■ ■ ■

Come, Lord Jesus, into our frayed and turning world and
redeem it and us with it. Amen.

January 29

Mark 1:19-20
As he went a little farther, he saw James son of Zebedee
and his brother John, who were in their boat mending the
nets. Immediately he called them; and they left their father
Zebedee in the boat with the hired men, and followed him.

■ ■ ■

Empty nests, when the children are not home anymore, no matter how the emptiness happens are unnerving and always life-altering moments. Those who once consumed hours of our days and energy from our souls suddenly take wing. Though they remain forever ours, they are also forever on a new path. It was no small thing that Zebedee was left in the boat with the workers who were not his sons. He would not likely see his sons again. Zebedee might well have died before knowing the deaths his sons would meet for the sake of belief in this Jesus. The cost and the importance of following Christ is measured in such moments.

■ ■ ■

Lord God, help us to be obedient to your will and follow you in this day. Amen.

January 30

Psalm 133:1
How very good and pleasant it is when kindred live
together in unity!

■ ■ ■

From the beginning of the history of the people of Israel, they were given a vision. The vision was that God would be their God and they would be God's people. They would be given a homeland and a legacy of generations. In the course of their history, they had moments when they saw that dream realized. Those moments were often short-lived, but even in the ashes of shattered dreams they were given again the vision of one people, one God, one home forever. The vision remains imbedded in the core of who we are as children of God. We long to be in unity with one another. We ache to have the tension and the walls that separate us torn down. Even when we cannot seem to reach out to each other still we press our noses to the window and hope. Emily Dickinson once wrote that "Hope is the thing with feathers that perches in the soul. It sings the tune without the words and never stops at all." We may not always know how to bring about unity amongst ourselves, but God keeps teaching us how to sing the song that dreams of it.

■ ■ ■

Lord God, We praise your name and sing your song of hope and unity. Amen.

January 31

Deuteronomy 18:19-20
Anyone who does not heed the words that the prophet shall speak in my name, I myself will hold accountable. But any prophet who speaks in the name of other gods, or who presumes to speak in my name a word that I have not commanded the prophet to speak-that prophet shall die. "

■ ■ ■

Accountable. I have a love/hate relationship with that word. I work well when deadlines or appointments on the calendar or personal reminders help to hold me accountable to responsibilities or promises. I have a poor track record on matters where I must be accountable to myself. I try to manipulate the process by making others responsible for reminding me. I assume I am off the hook when I fail to follow through. I manage to turn important things to do into a complicated series of unproductive thought processes. The relationship which the Lord offers to us is rather blissfully simple. We are accountable to God and God will hold us accountable. Some days I squirm like crazy that I have to answer to anyone. Most days I revel in the grace that abounds when I trust in the one to whom I am accountable.

■ ■ ■

Lord God, help us to take your word seriously, to honor it with our obedience and we ask for your grace to keep trying when we disappoint you. Amen.

February 1

Psalm 111:2-3
Great are the works of the Lord, studied by all who delight
in them. Full of honor and majesty is his work, and his
righteousness endures forever. He has gained renown by
his wonderful deeds

■ ■ ■

To be creative - in any medium - is to reflect a way in which
we were made in the image of God. We are wired to create
because we were created by the Creator. We create because
it is sown into the fabric of our souls by a Master Designer.
Whether we sew or paint or design a machine or shape a
program or a filing system or till soil or imagine
landscaping or make dinner, we are children of a vast
creative mind. The world is God's handiwork; but, oh, the
masterpiece that human beings are! We have only just
begun to plumb the depths of his genius in creating us.
There is a profound joy in having someone pad around
inside your heart admiring the maker's incredible
imagination. It is a humble privilege to be allowed to see
the work of the Lord in someone else.

■ ■ ■

Thank you, Lord, for the masterpieces that you send into
our lives every day. For each of them, we give you honor
and glory. Amen.

February 2

I Corinthians 8: 1,3
Now concerning food sacrificed to idols: we know that "all of us possess knowledge." Anyone who claims to know something does not yet have the necessary knowledge; but anyone who loves God is known by him.

■ ■ ■

This passage sent my head into this bizarre singing duel between The Beatles and Tina Turner - "All you need is love" vs. "What's love got to do with it?" For some Christians eating idol offerings was a challenge to their faith. For others, it didn't make any difference because idols are meaningless. Paul calls us to make the decision based not on sound thinking but love. If doing what we are doing is a problem for someone else, then rather than claim our liberty, we should consider the needs of others. The question of "what does love require?" is absolutely necessary. Love requires sacrifice. Sometimes it is the sacrifice of our own freedom. When we weary of sacrifice, we slump into a self-indulgent pool of pity. Even there, we find ourselves in the hands of one who bears the scars of his sacrifice for us in his hands.

■ ■ ■

Lord God, make love real and according to your will, let it be made real for others through us today. Amen.

February 3

Mark 1: 21-22
They went to Capernaum; and when the Sabbath came, he entered the synagogue and taught. They were astounded at his teaching, for he taught them as one having authority, and not as the scribes.

■ ■ ■

This is a tough culture for experts in any subject. Put an expert witness on the stand and there is always another expert to discredit their opinions. A talk show host introduces an expert in a field and other experts have a feeding frenzy of opinions. There was something different in Jesus' teaching that was immediately noteworthy and created the first major buzz around his ministry. "This guy sounds like he knows what he is talking about." In this politically correct age of not wanting to step on any religious or non-religious toes in conversation, we lose our credibility when we waffle. What we can do is that we can be authoritative on what we have seen and heard. We are the experts on our faith journey. I know that Jesus saves me, forgives me my sins, and grants me grace every day. On that I am an expert...with personal experience....so are you.

■ ■ ■

God grant us the wisdom and strength to claim the authority of our own faith journey and share it with others. Amen.

February 4

Matthew 18:21
Lord, if another member of the church sins against me, how often should I forgive?

■　■　■

Don Henley, a contemporary rock singer, asks in the lyrics of one of his songs, "How can love survive in such a graceless age?" The conclusion the song comes to is "I think it's about forgiveness." We all operate with some romanticized ideas of what love is. Even in our most callous thoughts, we know that our disappointments about love were born of our expectations. I believe that testifies to the image of God that exists in shadows within us. In our dreams, we know what love at its best might look like. Distorted by selfishness, love inside our humanity is fragile. Love gains its strength and power not from acts of perfection but by being surrounded by an atmosphere of forgiveness. We are incapable of loving perfectly. God gives us what we need, however, to make love work. We are given forgiveness. Grace begets grace. Love survives when we abandon perfection and embrace grace.

■　■　■

Lord of Love, thank you for forgiving us and making real our best dream of love. Amen.

February 5

Isaiah 40:30-31
Even youths will faint and be weary, and the young will fall
exhausted; but those who wait for the Lord shall renew
their strength, they shall mount up with wings like eagles,
they shall run and not be weary, they shall walk and not
faint.

■ ■ ■

I wish I could fly. I've been in a hot-air balloon twice - once
over the plains of Texas and another time over the Rockies.
The crisp air kisses your face and the world moves beneath
you as you fly and float above it. I have sat on the bow of a
900 ft. freighter with my legs dangling over the edge. The
bow is so far from the ship's engine, you can only hear the
sound of the wind. I imagined myself an albatross who
spends the majority of its life in the air over the open ocean.
We don't think of our daily lives as nearly that exhilarating.
We run and we get weary. We walk and we faint. We get
weak. Something there is, however, about the nature of our
God - to be in his presence is to see a glimpse of a bigger,
magnificent world and our strength to move around in that
world, even if only on foot, is renewed.

■ ■ ■

Lift us up, Lord, and help us know the power of your
steadfast love. Amen.

February 6

Psalm 147:9-11
He gives to the animals their food, and to the young ravens
when they cry. His delight is not in the strength of the
horse, nor his pleasure in the speed of a runner; but the
Lord takes pleasure in those who fear him, in those who
hope in his steadfast love.

■ ■ ■

I own a parrot who talks, but only when he feels like it. It is an eerie moment when he looks at me and says, "I want some food!" and sure enough, his dish is empty and I have been scolded by a small, feathered thing for not doing my job. Pets remind us that we are granted pieces of creation over which we have dominion. We care for them and they give us some degree of pleasure and entertainment, but especially they are devoted to the one who feeds and shelters them. That devotion may not be particularly warm and fuzzy, but loyal and consistent, at least. We are more than animals and our God is more than a divine pet owner. God gives us a place in his kingdom above the creatures and extends his love and his mission to us as his children.

■ ■ ■

For all creatures, great and small, Lord we give you thanks and well as for the privilege of dominion and the honor of your love. Amen.

37

February 7

Psalm 2:1-2
Why are the nations in an uproar? Why do the peoples
mutter empty threats? Why do the kings of the earth rise
up in revolt, and the princes plot together, against the Lord
and against his anointed?

■ ■ ■

One of the important rules of battle engagement is to know
your opponent. We need to know what we are up against. In
order to succeed, we need to know our enemy's strengths
and weaknesses. As we engage one another in conflict, we
draw our lines in the sands to mark where we will not let
anyone invade. More often than not, we don't see that the
boundaries we draw sometimes put us in opposition to God.
In our focus on the enemy, we forget who we are. When we
make God our enemy, we totally forget who we are truly up
against. Why we have to make everything a battle is
another mystery. Perhaps the most important rule of battle
is not to become our own enemy. We just don't know what
we would do with ourselves if we were at peace inside our
own skins and with God. It is a good thing God is patient.

■ ■ ■

Let there be peace on earth, Lord, and let it begin with me.
Amen.

February 8

2 Peter 1:18-19
We ourselves heard this voice come from heaven, while we
were with him on the holy mountain. So we have the
prophetic message more fully confirmed. You will do well to
be attentive to this as to a lamp shining in a dark place,
until the day dawns and the morning star rises in your
hearts.

■ ■ ■

A man had an idea for a light bulb and built a prototype but he could not get it to work. He brought it to Thomas Edison who had not thought of ever inventing a light bulb. He was working on other things like the phonograph (the great grandfather of the iPod for our younger readers). Edison got the bulb to work. Often in our lives, we need help getting our bulbs to work. We need to be able to see the light and be the appropriate vehicles for the light, so that others may see. The voices in the Bible are voices of those who wanted to help people like us. Those bearers of the light longed to help us in our journey. We do well to listen to their faithful voices.

■ ■ ■

Let our light so shine today, Lord. Amen.

February 9

Matthew 17:5-7
While he was still speaking, suddenly a bright cloud
overshadowed them, and from the cloud a voice said, "This
is my Son, the Beloved; with him I am well pleased; listen
to him!" When the disciples heard this, they fell to the
ground and were overcome by fear. But Jesus came and
touched them, saying, "Get up and do not be afraid."

■ ■ ■

God pulled up the blinds and let the disciples have a quick
glimpse of the sight and sounds of divine glory. Their
reaction was understandable. They hit the ground. They
were afraid. Jesus, however, did not bark at them from
afar, but came close to where they were cowering. He
touched them and addressed their immediate concern.
When we get too caught up in our own self-importance, we
often need reminders of the bigness of God to stop us in
tracks that are leading nowhere. It is good once in a while
to stare into the sun to remember we would never win a
stare-down contest with it. A little trembling and humility
is not a bad thing. God is also big enough to make himself
small so that he can put his arm around our shoulders and
tell us, "Everything will be okay."

■ ■ ■

Lord God, thank you for meeting us in our smallness.
Amen.

February 10

Genesis 3:6
So when the woman saw that the tree was good for food,
and that it was a delight to the eyes, and that the tree was
to be desired to make one wise, she took of its fruit and ate;
and she also gave some to her husband, who was with her,
and he ate.

■ ■ ■

I am constantly amazed at our ability to talk ourselves into doing just about anything. In the Genesis story, the woman got enticed by the snake who fed her with false information and she used its' lies to convince herself to disobey God. The man who did not participate in the discussion, but apparently overheard it all, was convinced without asking any questions. In the age of information that currently bombards our lives with a plethora of information, we now have the heightened challenge of determining what information is true. Whose voice do we trust to steer us away from the lies around us? Whose voice do we let become intimately a part of us so that we can even identify the lies we tell ourselves?

■ ■ ■

Holy God, enter into our minds and hearts so that we may always know the sound of truth. Amen.

41

February 11

Psalm 32:1-2
Happy are they whose transgressions are forgiven, and
whose sin is put away! Happy are they to whom the Lord
imputes no guilt, and in whose spirit there is no guile.

■ ■ ■

There is nothing in the world like the ease of a relationship
that is free of deceit, doubts, confusion, and especially guilt.
We only experience those relationships in joyful moments.
We quickly muddy the waters around our loved ones, co-
workers, and neighbors. We put distance between us to the
point we are too exhausted or too guilty to shorten. The
blessed work of any relationship is not in trying to achieve
perfection, but in quickly recognizing the problems,
confessing, and forgiving. So it is in our relationship with
God. The miracle of grace is that no matter how far we
stray from his presence, we always have the ticket home.
God stuffed the promise tickets in our pockets on our way
out the door even as we tried to run away from him.

■ ■ ■

Precious Lord, for the openness of your heart and your
willingness to forgive us relentlessly we give you thanks.
Amen.

February 12

Roman 5:18-19
Therefore just as one man's trespass led to condemnation
for all, so one man's act of righteousness leads to
justification and life for all. For just as by the one man's
disobedience the many were made sinners, so by the one
man's obedience the many will be made righteous.

■ ■ ■

It is by Jesus we are made right with God. So why are we
all trying so hard to do it ourselves? Perhaps it is like when
we go to the doctor's office. We have been told that the
disease we have will not kill us, but we will need to take
medication for the rest of our lives. We have just been given
the good news that we will live, but walk out of the doctor's
office feeling sad. The news that we need outside help
overshadows the news that we will live. We are so
infatuated with our personal freedom we are willing to let it
lead us to death. Without the cross of Christ, we are
hurdling toward oblivion every day. With Jesus crucified
and risen again, we are going to live and we can dare to love
beyond our own survival. I would rather be a slave to Christ
than hold on to a freedom that doesn't know the way home.

■ ■ ■

Holy God, may we choose life over death every day. Amen.

43

February 13

Matthew 4:3-4
The tempter came and said to him, "If you are the Son of God, command these stones to become loaves of bread." But he answered, "It is written, 'One does not live by bread alone, but by every word that comes from the mouth of God.'"

■ ■ ■

In a group discussion about Lent, one person suggested I give up the word "jazz" for Lent because I use it so often not only as a noun but a verb. It would certainly be a hardship to lose it from my vocabulary for even a week. As we discussed the purpose of Lenten sacrifice though, we agreed it was probably not the kind of sacrifice that truly strengthens our journey of faith. Discipline helps to strengthen our resolve especially in a time of temptation. Temptation identifies our weakness and heartlessly makes its appeal for our lives. By dangling the possibility of food in front of a hungry man, the devil sought to get Jesus to respond to his command. Rather than giving up a word for Lent, the discipline of feasting on God's Word every day is more powerful than we can imagine.

■ ■ ■

Lord, let the word that satisfies my hungry heart today be the name of your Son spoken at the moments when I feel the weakest. In the name of Jesus, Amen.

February 14

Genesis 12:1-3
The Lord said to Abram, "Go from your country and your kindred and your father's house to the land that I will show you. I will make of you a great nation, and I will bless you, and make your name great, so that you will be a blessing. I will bless those who bless you, and the one who curses you I will curse; and in you all the families of the earth shall be blessed.

■　■　■

When God said, "Go" to Abram, a series of events began. It moved through generations. It moved into new land. The shockwave of that "Go" would vibrate through the history of God's people until it would be stopped dead, impaled on a lonely cross on a hill outside of Jerusalem. Today is Valentine's Day - the celebration of love. No matter your situation in life the celebration of love in a world of sorrow is always a good thing. This story of God's promise was the beginning of God's Valentine to the world - love beyond all measure in the compassion of Jesus Christ. God's "Go" was resurrected and carries the blessing of God's love story that began so long and so far away includes you and me.

■　■　■

Loving God, send us with your love into a world which needs your love. Amen.

February 15

Psalm 121:5,8
The Lord himself watches over you; the Lord is your shade
at your right hand... The Lord shall watch over your going
out and your coming in, from this time forth forevermore.

■ ■ ■

When I went to the beach as a child with my family, I would need to be watched. Beyond obvious safety reasons, I needed to be watched because I couldn't wear my glasses in the ocean. The surf would always carry me down the beach from where the family blanket was located. I was oblivious of my location until I heard my name and a fuzzy image of some family member flagging me with a towel. It wasn't the first nor the last time I would have to be watched. It doesn't take much in the busy-ness of active days to forget where we are. We forget what we are doing. Sometimes we even forget who brought us. That the Lord has endured my lifetime of oblivious moments is certainly humbling. That he has enduring oblivious moments for all of humanity from the beginning of time ....gets my undivided attention.

■ ■ ■

Gracious God, thank you for your relentless watch. Through the constant waves of things to do, help me to hear my name in the wind and pay attention to your voice. Amen.

February 16

Romans 4:4-5
Now to one who works, wages are not reckoned as a gift but as something due. But to one who without works trusts him who justifies the ungodly, such faith is reckoned as righteousness.

■ ■ ■

Reckoned as righteousness. As easily as it falls off the tongue, it is equally difficult to understand. It is crucial that we do understand that our lives in relationship with God is not about perfection but faith. Even when we hear that, we quickly forget it until we desperately need to hear it again. How many times when working on a project which is not quite as perfect as I would like did I finally have to say...."Let's call it good." God simply does the same thing for us. He looks at sinners who are never going to be perfect who are looking to him for help and God takes the "looking part" and says...."Let's call it good." We can never create perfection or be perfect. The best we can do is recognize perfection when we see it in God and believe. It is in looking that God says, "Perfect!"

■ ■ ■

Gracious God, forgive me when I spin my wheels trying to achieve a perfection that is beyond my grasp and will not satisfy my deepest need. I need you, Lord. Thank you for coming to me and calling me good. Amen.

47

February 17

John 3:16-17
For God so loved the world that he gave his only Son, so that everyone who believes in him may not perish but may have eternal life. Indeed, God did not send the Son into the world to condemn the world, but in order that the world might be saved through him.

■ ■ ■

If we look for reasons to condemn other people, we will find reasons. What annoys us about people are often small matters, as small as hangnails, but like a hangnail we chew at it until it bleeds. What have we accomplished in cutting others down to size is to leave ourselves isolated and delusional. We have left others bleeding. Through the blood of Christ, we are given a new way to live. We can choose to think on those things which are true, honest, just, pure, praiseworthy. We can still choose to acknowledge one another's faults and short-comings and love one another nonetheless. We can actually do that because God so loved the world.

■ ■ ■

Holy God, I believe that you know everything about me and love me nonetheless. Amen.

February 18

Exodus 17: 4-6
So Moses cried out to the Lord, "What shall I do with this
people? They are almost ready to stone me." The Lord said
to Moses, "Go on ahead of the people, and take some of the
elders of Israel with you; take in your hand the staff with
which you struck the Nile, and go. I will be standing there
in front of you on the rock at Horeb. Strike the rock, and
water will come out of it, so that the people may drink.

■ ■ ■

The people are thirsty and seem angry enough to Moses to
want to hit him. Instead of allowing people to start
throwing stones at Moses, God invites Moses to hit a rock.
Interesting twist. Moses gets to vent his frustration AND
the people get water AND they all get another sign of God's
power and provision AND Moses' leadership is kept intact.
Our conflicts and problems aren't often resolved with that
much tactical brilliance. We tend to go off on tangents,
think with our stomachs, and blame whoever is close by and
thrash in anger. So that we might live, God offers us
something on which we can take out our frustrations. When
we are finished venting, there is a man dead on a cross.

■ ■ ■

Lord God, make us bold to take to the cross our hurt and
frustration so that we might deal tenderly with one another
and live in peace, trusting in your forgiveness and mercy.
Amen.

February 19

Psalm 95:7-9
For he is our God, and we are the people of his pasture and the sheep of his hand. Oh, that today you would hearken to his voice. Harden not your hearts, as your forebears did in the wilderness, at Meribah, and on that day at Massah, when they tempted me. They put me to the test though they had seen my works.

■ ■ ■

The comedian Bill Cosby does a monologue about how children never respond to anything said the first time. "Come here....pause...come HERE....shorter pause...COME HERE!!!" In a classroom, students know if they wait long enough after the teacher asks a question that the teacher will eventually answer the question him or herself. It is enough to wear thin the patience of anyone. God is infinitely patient, but it doesn't mean God likes having to wade through our layers of thick cluelessness. We may choose to be attentive because we are afraid of God's wrath, but God would prefer that we were attentive for the same reason he is attentive to us - because he cares.

■ ■ ■

Gracious God, forgive us for our oblivious nature. Clean our ears that we might hear you through the din of other voices. Today we hope we don't make you work so hard. Amen.

February 20

Romans 5: 3-5
And not only that, but we also boast in our sufferings,
knowing that suffering produces endurance, and endurance
produces character, and character produces hope, and hope
does not disappoint us, because God's love has been poured
into our hearts through the Holy Spirit that has been given
to us.

■ ■ ■

It occurred to me yesterday that nowhere in the Apostles' Creed (which is a statement of the basics of the faith dating back to the 3rd century) does it ever mention the word love. Somewhere along the way in our lives we have gotten the idea that love exists as an entity by itself in the world, but apart from God, love is something less than the whole truth. We believe in God the Creator who loved the world he created. We believe in Christ who loved us so much that he died for us. We believe in the Holy Spirit that gives us a capacity to love and forgive one another beyond our sinful ability to do so. Apart from that God, we can play at love but no one does love better than Jesus. The Holy Spirit helps us get a clue. Our statement of faith may not mention love specifically but it is all about love.

■ ■ ■

Lord God, hold on to us. Recreate us. Pour your Spirit into us so that we might be signs of your gracious love. Amen.

February 21

John 4:10-11
Jesus answered her, "If you knew the gift of God, and who it is that is saying to you, 'Give me a drink,' you would have asked him, and he would have given you living water." The woman said to him, "Sir, you have no bucket, and the well is deep. Where do you get that living water?

■ ■ ■

One of the great mistakes we have in our relationship with God is that we think too much inside the box. We make God too small. The woman couldn't think outside the bucket. We need buckets and boxes and rules in order to function, but sometimes it is very important to think outside those lines. Jesus gave the woman a glimpse of something bigger than a quenched thirst. He gave her an overflowing life. God works on us from the outside in and from the inside out to reveal his true nature which is unfathomable grace. God could think outside the box because even though he created the box, what he did outside the box was genius.

■ ■ ■

Awesome God, when we are unable to see the forest for the trees grant us the courage and grace to view the world from your Son. Amen.

February 22

Psalm 130:1-3
Out of the depths have I called to you, O Lord; Lord, hear
my voice; let your ears consider well the voice of my
supplication. If you, Lord, were to note what is done amiss,
O Lord, who could stand? For there is forgiveness with you;
therefore you shall be feared. I wait for the Lord; my soul
waits for him; in his word is my hope.

■ ■ ■

Do you ever have those days when there isn't a reason under God's green earth why you should feel like you are standing in a hole, but there you are? Talking to myself never works. If anything, I am too good at convincing myself that I truly deserve to be in that hole, so I should just get comfortable. When I consider the history of the Lord in my life I know that the hole isn't where God has ever left me. Talking with God always helps. I like to think that the letters in the word LENT means the Lord's Ears Never Tire. God's love and forgiveness is always like a rope thrown down to us.

■ ■ ■

Hear us, O Lord, when we call out to you from the pits we get ourselves into. Listen to us in our loneliness and lift us up to do your will in the world. Amen.

February 23

I Corinthians 9:22-23
To the weak I became weak, so that I might win the weak. I have become all things to all people, that I might by all means save some. I do it all for the sake of the gospel, so that I may share in its blessings.

■ ■ ■

If we didn't know anything about Paul and his ministry, we would say he is just another pompous preacher, full of himself and snatching after the power and the glory of a trendy, new religion. What he was, in his heart and soul, was a person who ached for others to know Jesus. He saw the hurting, misled, wandering, rootless church of Corinth and shouted out to them...."I am here for you. Look at me. I will sacrifice my identity in order to reach you with God's good news for you." Paul loved God and he loved God's people and he trusted that the blessings of the gospel would also be his. That kind of commitment and integrity in the ministry seems rare these days in the midst of clergy misconduct and puffed-up television evangelists. But God continues to speak through the lives of ordinary men and women for the sake of the gospel.....God will make that voice heard.

■ ■ ■

Holy God, grant us the compassion and the courage to lose ourselves so that others may know your grace. Amen.

February 24

Mark 1:35-37
In the morning, while it was still very dark, he got up and went out to a deserted place, and there he prayed. And Simon and his companions hunted for him. When they found him, they said to him, "Everyone is searching for you."

■ ■ ■

I know a person whose life is kinetic with the activity of an active household of children. Some days she is able to rise in the early morning, sit in a chair near her bed, read her Bible and pray in the stillness before her family stirs. Those moments happen rarely. Her prayers are more often what she calls "shooter" prayers - said on the fly but nonetheless earnest and heartfelt. The beat of her day is filled with phone calls and schedules and interruptions and a wild mix of endless details and tender mercies. Jesus modeled the same life of ministry and prayer. Some days praying in the stillness....other days on the road doing his Father's will. The interruptions were as much a part of the fabric of his time as what he was doing intentionally. God means for us to be truly immersed in ministry in such a way that we are endlessly in conversation and in his presence.

■ ■ ■

Every minute of every day, Lord, make us keenly aware of your presence and your will. Amen.

February 25

2 Kings 5:13-14
But his servants approached and said to him, "Father, if the
prophet had commanded you to do something difficult,
would you not have done it? How much more, when all he
said to you was, 'Wash, and be clean'?" So he went down
and immersed himself seven times in the Jordan, according
to the word of the man of God; his flesh was restored like
the flesh of a young boy, and he was clean.

■ ■ ■

Naaman, a commander of a great army, was angry that the
prophet had not made a personal appearance to cure him,
but rather told him to wash in the Jordan. He thought his
rank deserved some more one on one attention. That he was
asking for a miracle got lost in the cacophony of his own
ego. His servants had to be the ones to give him a wake-up
call. There is a fine line between poor self-esteem, personal
confidence, and rampaging self-importance. Some people
hate to think about it and so get stuck in one extreme or the
other. Everything we have and everything we are is a gift,
and the one who gives us everything loves us with mad
abandon. Somehow, remembering that every day helps to
keep us from becoming a burden or a bore or a fool.

■ ■ ■

Lord God, we humbly ask for your help in remembering the
miracle of just being alive in your love. Amen.

February 26

Psalm 30:11-12
You have turned my wailing into dancing; you have put off
my sackcloth and clothed me with joy. Therefore my heart
sings to you without ceasing; O Lord my God, I will give you
thanks forever.

■ ■ ■

I can safely say that I have never wailed. I do admit that I
have white-knuckled my way through more than one
airplane take-off. I admit that I have, on occasion, lifted my
feet as if to help the plane up. Flying seems so unnatural
and yet, if you talk to a pilot, it is the most natural thing in
the world. What helps me settle back in my seat is the last
verse of Matthew...."Lo, I am with you always to the end of
the age." It simply doesn't get any better than that. God is
with us. Everything will be all right. We have a reason to
sing and give thanks every day.

■ ■ ■

Through our fears, Lord, help us to trust and sing. Amen.

February 27

I Corinthians 9:25-26
Athletes exercise self-control in all things; they do it to
receive a perishable wreath, but we can imperishable one.
So I do not run aimlessly, nor do I box as though beating at
the air.

■ ■ ■

These are verses that make us stop and think while we are
in the middle of running aimlessly or flailing away at a "to
do" list that grows longer as we flail. It is a good thing to
consider why we are doing what we are doing once in a
while. Sometimes the answer is simple - we are mowing the
lawn because the lawn needs mowing. Other times, the
answers might be more complex. We may do something for
the glory of God or just to feel at peace inside our own skin.
The life of a disciple is one of discipline, sacrifice, and living
life inside out. The reason why we do it may be gloriously
noble or plainly self-serving but God rewards us with the
promise that our efforts will not be in vain.

■ ■ ■

Holy God, Help us to run the race set before us and to
remember the promise of victory in you. Amen.

February 28

Isaiah 43:18-19
Do not remember the former things, or consider the things
of old. I am about to do a new thing; now it springs forth, do
you not perceive it? I will make a way in the wilderness and
rivers in the desert.

■　■　■

The organist in the church in which I grew up sat at the
organ console with her back to the congregation. She had a
rear-view mirror positioned so that she could see
everything. She stayed there through the whole service
even though she could have moved to a nearby chair or pew.
I don't know who deserved more sympathy - this woman
who was always looking backward or the pastor who was
always preaching to her backside. There is a good time for
remembering and a good time to set one's face toward the
future. It is all in the timing, but the future takes priority
for it is filled with the next brilliant brush strokes of our
creative God for the sake of the world.

■　■　■

Holy God, point us forward so that strengthened by the
wisdom of the past we may serve you faithfully in the
future. Amen.

February 29

Psalm 41:11-13
By this I know you are pleased with me; that my enemy
does not triumph over me, in my integrity you hold me fast,
and set me before your face forever. Blessed be the Lord
God of Israel from age to age. Amen.

■ ■ ■

How I love that word "integrity." In a time when we have a
tendency to compartmentalize our lives and lean toward
situational ethics, the call of integrity is a different call
indeed. Integrity beckons us to integrate. It bids us know
our values, embrace truth, and live honestly without having
to shove aside, spin doctor, ignore, or betray our cherished
beliefs. Often when the word integrity is mentioned in the
scriptures, it is used with the word "walk" ‐ we walk with
integrity when we don't have separate sets of values for
different areas of our lives. We walk the talk. The word
integrity is rarely ever used in the New Testament because
the word is made flesh in the person of Jesus. Jesus did not
ignore or dismiss our sinful nature, but took it on himself.
The resurrection was the outcome of the sin and death and
God's grace and forgiveness. God keeps the integrity of his
word intact in the body and blood of his Son's death and
resurrection.

■ ■ ■

May we be people of integrity in living your love and grace.
Amen.

60

March 1

2 Corinthians 1:21-22
But it is God who establishes us with you in Christ and has anointed us, by putting his seal on us and giving us his Spirit in our hearts as a first installment.

■ ■ ■

We were marked with the cross of Christ at our baptism. We are to be known as Christ's servants in the world, but that mark needs to sink through our pores to course through our veins. The mark needs to invade the marrow of our bones and fire the synapses of our brain and warm our hearts. This is the sign to us of our lives returned to us. It is returned to us, however, in such a way that we will know that no matter how much brokenness, loss, disappointments, sufferings, death we have known - the mark for us will always mean that we are marked for life *for life*.

■ ■ ■

Holy God, sink into our hearts and minds so that we may be convinced of our grace and become a living sign of your promises kept. Amen.

March 2

Mark 2:10-12
But so that you may know that the Son of Man has
authority on earth to forgive sins - he said to the paralytic -
I say to you, stand up, take your mat and go to your home.
And he stood up, and immediately took the mat and went
out before all of them; so that they were all amazed and
glorified God, saying, "We have never seen anything like
this!"

■ ■ ■

Forgiveness is absolutely essential to our lives together and
we are often rather pitiful at it. We might say the words but
they fall empty on the floor. We may make a gesture but
plot to make the other pay for the hurt they have caused.
We are all terrible at forgetting. The forgiveness God offers
to us makes our feeble efforts pale in comparison. His
forgiveness is utterly complete, perfectly sound, totally
whole. Our powerful God has the ability to choose to forget
and make brand new that which we might only be able to
re-furbish. When the disciples said that they have never
seen anything like the power of Jesus to forgive - neither
have we. Jesus takes the puny crumbs of our confession and
forgiveness and makes it more than good enough.

■ ■ ■

Holy God, forgive us and teach us to forgive. Amen.

March 3

Psalm 133:1
How very good and pleasant it is when kindred live
together in unity!

■　■　■

From the beginning of the history of the people of Israel, they were given a vision. The vision was that God would be their God and they would be God's people. They would be given a homeland and a legacy of generations. In the course of their history, they had moments when they saw that dream realized. Those moments were often short-lived but even in the ashes of shattered dreams they were given again the vision of one people, one God, one home forever. The vision remains imbedded in the core of who we are as children of God. We long to be in unity with one another. We ache to have the tension and the walls that separate us torn down. Even when we cannot seem to reach out to each other still we press our noses to the window and hope. Emily Dickinson once wrote that "Hope is a thing of feathers that perches in the soul. It sings the tune without the words and never stops at all." We may not always know how to bring about unity amongst ourselves but God keeps teaching us how to sing the song that dreams of it.

■　■　■

Lord God, we praise your name and sing your song of hope and unity. Amen.

March 4

John 19:39
Nicodemus, who had at first come to Jesus by night, also
came.

■ ■ ■

Nicodemus was a man of shadows. We know little about him except for his faith struggles. He was a member of the group of Jewish leaders who were opposed to Jesus' teachings. But there was something about this Jesus that compelled Nicodemus to steal away from his colleagues and in the cover of darkness go to Jesus. He asked him questions that betrayed his hunger to believe and his doubt. Nicodemus disappeared into the night with more questions than when he came. And yet, Nicodemus appears again. Lurking in the shadows of the crucified Christ, he offers the spices and materials needed to prepare his body for burial. Was it a gesture motivated by guilt or devotion or both? Perhaps Nicodemus was the first worshiper on Good Fridays. For centuries to come, the character of Nicodemus stands with us in the shadows with our own guilt, our own devotion and together with look to Christ with hope.

■ ■ ■

God of Hope, even in the finality of the death of your Son, you give us reason to believe in life. Amen.

March 5

Psalm 50:1-2
The mighty one, God the Lord, speaks and summons the earth from the rising of the sun to its setting. Out of Zion, the perfection of beauty, God shines forth.

■ ■ ■

In the fuzzy memories of my smallest childhood, I remember sitting in, what was to me, a huge over-stuffed chair. My feet stuck out, but did not even dangle off the edge. I would have had to put my arms over my head to place my hands on the armrests. I sat comfortably in the shadows and felt marvelously safe. I own some chairs today that are probably the same size as that chair was only now I am bigger. I cannot hide anymore especially from the presence and the will of God. Sometimes God is just so big that we are only aware of our own puniness. But there is great comfort and joy in reveling in the majesty of God when we know that we are saved and safe, surrounded by his grace and love.

■ ■ ■

Almighty God, we sit easy in your grace. Amen.

March 6

2 Corinthians 4:5-6
For we do not proclaim ourselves; we proclaim Jesus Christ as Lord and ourselves as your slaves for Jesus' sake. For it is the God who said, "Let light shine out of darkness," who has shown in our hearts to give the light of the knowledge of the glory of God in the face of Jesus Christ.

■ ■ ■

Here lies the dilemma. On the one hand, we are driven by the longing to belong to something greater than ourselves. We want to know that we are unique and valued in a complex but glorious movement. On the other hand, we resist being just a cog in a wheel. We desire to be independent and appreciated for who we are individually, not just for our part in the whole. We are caught between a rock and a hard place. And both the rock and the hard place have our names on them. Both desires are driven by our belief that we should determine our own meaning and value. Moving from the inside out, God shines through our lives, calls us to die to self and live in the knowledge that we are joyfully, utterly and completely, his. In God's kingdom, the rock and the hard place disappear.

■ ■ ■

Shine, Jesus, shine and let others see your grace through us today. Amen.

March 7

Genesis 9:16-17
When the bow is in the clouds, I will see it and remember
the everlasting covenant between God and every living
creature of all flesh that is on the earth. God said to Noah,
"This is the sign of the covenant that I have established
between me and all flesh that is on the earth.

■ ■ ■

I have taken a couple trips by booking passage on container ships that have extra cabin space for passengers. On one of my freighter trips, there was an occasion when I was on deck, The air was filled will moisture and sea mist. A rainbow appeared in the air where I was standing - so close I could put my hand in it. It made me laugh out loud all by myself like a thoroughly delighted child. Lots of different political action groups in recent years have embraced the rainbow as a sign of unity in the midst of diversity. However, it will always be for me a sign of God's crayolian imagination and deep promise to extend grace to his people. He gives us signs in the midst of tumult that his covenant with us is a done deal.

■ ■ ■

Lord, help us to see and recognize the signs of your kingdom today. Amen.

March 8

Psalm 23:4-5
Though I walk through the valley of the shadow of death, I shall fear no evil; for you are with me; your rod and your staff, they comfort me. You spread a table before me in the presence of those who trouble me; you have anointed my head with oil, and my cup is running over.

■ ■ ■

We are all in this together. The psalmist was in the temple with the people who were driving him nuts. More than likely, people telling him that he wasn't quite as good as they were and generously pointing out his flaws. Why do we do that to one another? This psalm is wonderfully comforting, but what if someone today is praying this psalm because we are the ones who are troubling them? I have been much more abundantly changed by those who have accepted me as I am than by those who revel in pointing out to me what I already know - I am flawed. The ones who trouble others lead lonely lives. The ones who are troubled walk in the company of the Almighty.

■ ■ ■

Holy God, help us today to seize the moment to lift up rather than trouble another on the journey we share. Amen.

March 9

Ephesians 5: 14
For everything that becomes visible is light. Therefore it
says, "Sleeper, awake! Rise from the dead, and Christ will
shine on you. "

■ ■ ■

I attended a church camp in New Hampshire in my teenage days. They hung speakers on the trees between the cabins and played Bach's "Sleepers Awake" instead of a bugle call to get us out of bed. It was the best invitation to a new day I have ever heard with the exception of Easter. We wake every day into an Easter promise. We arise to grace and mercy of a new day in which we can be the children of God. Christ shines from the inside out so that we might be light even on dark, gray days. Shine, Jesus, Shine.

■ ■ ■

Lord God, for the grace of a good night's sleep, for another day to serve you, for the people who shine on our darkness and wake our sleepy faith, we give you thanks. Amen.

March 10

John 9:35-36
Jesus heard that they had driven him out, and when he found him, he said, "Do you believe in the Son of Man?" He answered, "And who is he, sir? Tell me, so that I may believe in him."

■ ■ ■

The part of the verse today that leaped out at me was "when he found him." Jesus went looking for the man who had been healed of his blindness, but now needed compassion. We don't find Christ. Christ finds us. Even at times in our lives when we feel the most misunderstood, isolated, ashamed, hidden - there is Christ seeking us out. A survival skill in the wilderness is that if we are lost, it is better to stay put than wander aimlessly and lose energy needed to survive. Hopefully, those who know we are missing will be looking for us. Sometimes when we feel lost in our relationship with God, it is best to stay put and wait with hope. God will find us.

■ ■ ■

Lord God, your love always finds a way. Teach us to wait with patience. Amen.

March 11

I Samuel 16:6-7
When they came, he looked on Eliab and thought, "Surely
the Lord's anointed is now before the Lord." But the Lord
said to Samuel, "Do not look on his appearance or on the
height of his stature, because I have rejected him; for the
Lord does not see as mortals see; they look on the outward
appearance, but the Lord looks on the heart. "

■ ■ ■

I am beginning to believe that we misunderstand one
another more often than we understand one another. We
hear only what we want to hear through a clogged filter. We
see only what lays on the surface. To understand one
another takes a great deal of work and a change of heart -
the desire to look again past our own agenda to the person
God places before us. To understand means to package
away our first impressions, our prejudices, our own anger
or disappointments and allow that person to stand inside
what the theologian Henri Nouwen described as "friendly,
empty space." And that is only the beginning of
understanding, grace and love.

■ ■ ■

Lord God, make us aware this day of the friendly, empty
space that surrounds us, allowing us to be who we are and
loved nonetheless. Change our hearts so that we might offer
that same space to others. Amen.

March 12

Romans 8:11
If the Spirit of him who raised Jesus from the dead dwells
in you, he who raised Christ from the dead will give life to
your mortal bodies also through his Spirit that dwells in
you.

■ ■ ■

There is a song from the musical Auntie Mame in which
during the month of June, Mame sings "We need a little
Christmas...." Well, sometimes we need a little Easter right
this very minute. Since the spirit of the one who raised
Jesus from the dead dwells in us, then there is a power
within us that is mind-boggling. We will only know the
extent of that power when we ourselves are raised from the
dead and reunited with all the saints who have gone before
us. I am convinced, however, we get glimpses of little
Easters whenever the children of God do random acts of
kindness, love with mad abandon or take a stand for justice.

■ ■ ■

Lord, arise in our hearts. Awaken our spirit and show us
flashes of your Easter power in the love and mercy that
courses through our lives for others. Amen.

March 13

John 11:14-16
Then Jesus told them plainly, "Lazarus is dead. For your
sake I am glad I was not there, so that you may believe. But
let us go to him. " Thomas, who was called the Twin, said to
his fellow disciples, "Let us also go, that we may die with
him. "

■ ■ ■

If Thomas was a twin, where was the other one? It occurred
to me this morning - WE are Thomas' twin! All Thomas saw
was grief and death. All that a person can do with a dead
man is grieve with the family and lie down in the loss. That
is all Thomas could see and we wouldn't see anything
different than our brother. Jesus sees an opportunity for
faith to sprout. Jesus sees God's power. Jesus sees life. It is
easier to be Thomas' twin than Jesus' twin, but the world
needs more people cherishing life than embracing death.
Thomas figured that out eventually too.

■ ■ ■

Give us, Lord, the eyes to see and celebrate life blooming
around and in us that we might grow hope and be Christ
alive for one another. Amen.

March 14

Isaiah 50:4
The Lord has given me the tongue of a teacher, that I may
know how to sustain the weary with a word. Morning by
morning he wakens- wakens my ear to listen as those who
are taught.

■ ■ ■

The process of teaching is one not just one of spouting information, but it also involves the fine art of saying the best word at the best moment. And it also means knowing when to listen and learn. We never stop being students. The best teachers I know are the ones who keep learning. The wizard Merlin of the King Arthur stories said, "When you are sad, learn something." In my own experience, every lesson, especially of God's tender care and trustworthiness, has brought me joy.

■ ■ ■

We thank you, Lord, for those who teach us your word and who listen so well. Amen.

March 15

Psalm 31:13-14
For I have heard the whispering of the crowd; fear is all around; they put their heads together against me; they plot to take my life. But as for me, I have trusted in you, O Lord. I have said, "You are my God."

■ ■ ■

Trust works better as an action verb than it does a noun. If it is a noun, then trust is something we either have or not. Trust, like love, is more clearly recognized as an act of will. When we are trusting in our relationship with God, there is a power coursing through our veins for the sake of a relationship. Those who trust by taking a leap and those who trust by walking over rocks and moving mountains to keep living in God's direction are blessed with a history of God's faithfulness that makes trusting more like breathing.

■ ■ ■

Lord God, for all the times you have kept us from falling and given us the strength to overcome obstacles, we give you thanks. Amen.

March 16

Philippians 2:9-10
Therefore God also highly exalted him and gave him the
name that is above every name, so that at the name of
Jesus every knee should bend, in heaven and on earth and
under the earth.

■ ■ ■

I have been near-sighted since I was 7 years old. Since then I have needed glasses to correct my out-of-focus world. I discovered once that I could see a little spot at a distance without my glasses if I looked through a tiny hole made in a piece of paper. The biology and the physics of it all had something to do with what the eye was being forced to do. As Christians, we are drawn toward one small focal point. One moment in time, one tiny spot on a map of the world, one human being. With the cross of Christ as our focal point, the world and our place in it becomes clear.

■ ■ ■

Jesus, Savior, focusing on you and your cross, may we walk more clearly in your ways. Amen.

March 17

Genesis 3:8-9
They heard the sound of the Lord God walking in the
garden at the time of the evening breeze, and the man and
his wife hid themselves from the presence of the Lord God
among the trees of the garden. But the Lord God called to
the man, and said to him, "Where are you?"

■ ■ ■

Robert Frost wrote: "We make ourselves a place apart behind light words that tease and flout but oh, the agitated heart 'til someone finds us really out...and so with all the babes that play at hide-n-seek to God afar so those who hide too well away must speak and tell us where they are." As the spring of the year draws closer, let us attend to our hiding places. Let us consider why we have distanced ourselves from the One we need the most. Let us find the source of our sorrow and shame. But let us also listen for the voice of the One who has himself known the loneliness of wondering if he was all alone in the world. Let us prepare to answer the question of the One who seeks to save us - "Where are you?"

■ ■ ■

Holy God, we give you thanks for your relentless
willingness to come to us, look for us, call us out of our
hiding places so that we can find ourselves in you. Amen.

77

March 18

John 18: 37-38
Pilate asked him, "So you are a king?" Jesus answered,
"You say that I am a king. For this I was born, and for this I
came into the world, to testify to the truth. Everyone who
belongs to the truth listens to my voice." Pilate asked him,
"What is truth?"

■ ■ ■

There is no record of Jesus answering Pilate's question about the truth. He didn't have to. The truth was standing in front of him. Maybe it glimmered for a moment in Pilate's sight. Perhaps for a moment he was just another lost one seeking to find his way home. If such a moment ever happened, it didn't last long. Pilate went back to work. I believe God enters into our lives every day with the truth. It may come on the wings of that which we least expect, but when we are looking, it is right there in front of us.

■ ■ ■

Lord God, open us to the truth. Help us to see it in your face as you set your face toward the cross. Amen.

March 19

John 19:26-27
When Jesus saw his mother and the disciple whom he loved standing beside her, he said to his mother, "Woman, here is your son." Then he said to the disciple, "Here is your mother." And from that hour the disciple took her into his own home.

■ ■ ■

John Updike wrote, "Westerners have lost whole octaves of passion. Third world women can still make an inhuman piercing grieving noise right from the floor of the soul." Women were rarely allowed to speak in public, in Jesus' day, but they were allowed in grief to wail. I wonder if Jesus heard the cries of these women from his cross. In this sublime gesture, even in his own pain, he reaches out to them with mercy. The commandment to honor one's mother and father was never so completely and beautifully kept in one moment in time.

■ ■ ■

Lord God, for your unfailing love and your obedient heart, we give you thanks and praise. Amen.

March 20

Matthew 26:26-28
While they were eating, Jesus took a loaf of bread, and after blessing it he broke it, gave it to the disciples, and said, "Take, eat; this is my body." Then he took a cup, and after giving thanks he gave it to them, saying, "Drink from it, all of you; for this is my blood of the covenant, which is poured out for many for the forgiveness of sins."

■　■　■

In Christendom there has been much written and many have debated about what happens to bread and wine at communion. Some say it ceases to be bread and wine and becomes body and blood. Some say it is only a symbol. Some say it is something in between. I wonder if we have not wearied our Lord. At the first communion that was Jesus' last supper, he was saying goodbye to people with whom he had traveled for almost 4 years. He knew within hours they would break his heart and deny they were ever friends. Even still, that night, he lifted bread and wine and promised forgiveness to them. We may differ in our thoughts about when or if or how bread becomes Jesus, but he still said this is my body...take and eat...this is for you.

■　■　■

Lord, feed us with yourself that we might live to embrace your mercy and love as you do. Amen.

March 21

Acts 2:23-24
This man, handed over to you according to the definite plan and foreknowledge of God, you crucified and killed by the hands of those outside the law. But God raised him up, having freed him from death, because it was impossible for him to be held in its power.

■ ■ ■

In two words, the Gospel of the Risen Christ breaks into our week. "But God...." We crucify. We kill. It is our sin that laid Jesus low. BUT GOD....raised him from the dead. We betray. We forget. We get angry. We argue. BUT GOD...loves and forgives us. We ache. We fear. We doubt. BUT GOD....remains faithful and promises us life everlasting. No matter what we bring into this day, there is a comma and a "But God...." at the end of it to give us a promise of yet another new day.

■ ■ ■

Risen Lord, surprise us with your voice, your presence and your dazzling grace. Amen.

March 22

Psalm 16: 8,11
I have set the Lord always before me; because he is at my
right hand, I shall not fall. You will show me the path of
life; in your presence there is fullness of joy and in your
right hand are pleasures forevermore.

■ ■ ■

I went to New Zealand to hike the Milford track. The park
service only allows one group of people on the track per day
and three guides are assigned to each group. There was the
rear guide who I got to know quite well! There was the
middle guide who was strong as an ox and could carry extra
backpacks when needed. And there was the front guide who
was always the swiftest. The front guide was called the
"party guide" because that one had our refreshments
waiting for us as we walked in the door of the track hut for
the night. The resurrected Lord is all three! He picks up the
rear and walks at the pace of those who are tired and slow.
He carries our load. He prepares a party at our journey's
end.

■ ■ ■

"Guide me ever, Great Redeemer, pilgrim through this
barren land. I am weak but you are mighty. Hold me with
your powerful hand." Amen.

82

March 23

I Peter 1:8-9
Although you have not seen him, you love him; and even though you do not see him now, you believe in him and rejoice with an indescribable and glorious joy, for you are receiving the outcome of your faith, the salvation of your souls.

■ ■ ■

In Philippians, Paul echoed Peter's words by saying "I am confident of this, that the one who began a good work among you will bring it to completion by the day of Jesus Christ. " There is a group of women I know who gather every week to work on craft projects including a quilt that is sold for charity every year. Every project they do is different and in different stages ....but always they have a work in process. We are our Lord's work in process. God is transforming us from the inside out. There are plenty of days when we have absolutely no indication of that. There are also plenty of days when a smile creeps across our face for reasons we can only claim as divine joy.

■ ■ ■

"Joyful, joyful we adore thee, God of Glory, Lord of Love! Hearts unfold like flow'rs before thee, praising thee, their sun above.." Amen.

March 24

John 20:30-31
Now Jesus did many other signs in the presence of his
disciples, which are not written in this book. But these are
written so that you may come to believe that Jesus is the
Messiah, the Son of God, and that through believing you
may have life in his name.

■ ■ ■

John could have gone on and on but he picked the stories
purposefully for us, not for entertainment value or to make
his book a "great read." John wrote a Gospel so that we
might believe and have life. John was likely an old man
looking at the end of his time on this side of God's kingdom
when he wrote his Gospel. What would it mean for us to
end our careers and lives well? John decided to leave
something behind. He left a bunch of letters with stories of
Jesus so that others might believe and have life in his
name.

■ ■ ■

Help us, Lord, to keep telling the stories that were so
wonderfully told to us. Amen.

March 25

Psalm 25:1-2
To you, O Lord, I lift up my soul; my God, I put my trust in you; let me not be humiliated, nor let my enemies triumph over me. Let none who look to you be put to shame; let the treacherous be disappointed in their schemes.

■ ■ ■

The Milford Track in New Zealand is touted as the "finest walk in the world." It is grand in its vistas, meandering paths along mountain streams, majestic peaks, rainforest and ocean views. What they don't say in the travel brochures is that sometimes the path doesn't look like a path at all. Sometimes the way is a pile of rocks or a rushing river or a waving rope bridge or a ledge of shifting shale. No matter how clear or messy the path, we have to move forward with only our guts as our guide. When we walk by faith, we trust that God can use the offering of our contrite hearts and steer us toward his will.

■ ■ ■

Holy God, walk with us and guide us in your paths alone. Amen.

March 26

I Peter 3:21-22
And baptism...now saves you - not as a removal of dirt from
the body, but as an appeal to God for a good conscience,
through the resurrection of Jesus Christ, who has gone into
heaven and is at the right hand of God, with angels,
authorities, and powers made subject to him.

■ ■ ■

Our baptism has power to grant forgiveness of sins and
eternal life, because God chooses to make so. During a
baptism when I run my fingers through the water during
what I call- Luther's great "water" prayer, I am grateful
that God chose such a basic and readily available element
as a sign of his grace. There is nothing that keeps us from
having access to God's gifts because God in his authority,
chooses to make it accessible. He makes life accessible
through the death and the resurrection of his Son. Our
spiritual journey is sanctioned, authorized, and guided by
the spirit of the Living God.

■ ■ ■

Splashing in the waters of our baptism every day, we rejoice
again, O Lord, in your power and grace. Amen.

March 27

Mark 1:14-15
Now after John was arrested, Jesus came to Galilee,
proclaiming the good news of God, and saying, "The time is
fulfilled, and the kingdom of God has come near; repent,
and believe in the good news."

■ ■ ■

Everyone has pieces of songs that get stuck in their heads. I was asked one day what music tends to go through my head. Usually it is the line from a recent choir anthem or a hymn or, far worse, the sound of my alarm clock or cell phone tunes. Sometimes I will attempt to choose those brain tunes more intentionally. The ones I want to choose are Easter songs. In the weeks before Easter, we attend to our sinful selves and to the cross of Christ, his suffering and death. We also silence the word "Alleluia" until Easter morning. But "Alleluia"-like God's love and grace - cannot be kept silent.

■ ■ ■

Break us out of old habits, Lord, and fill us to overflowing with your alleluias. Amen.

March 28

Malachi 3:2-3
But who can endure the day of his coming, and who can stand when he appears? For he is like a refiner's fire and like fullers' soap; he will sit as a refiner and purifier of silver, and he will purify the descendants of Levi and refine them like gold and silver, until they present offerings to the Lord in righteousness.

■ ■ ■

Purity is a dream like perfection is a dream. We know we are not perfect, nor ever will be perfect, and yet there is a dream of it. We think that if we can dream it, then it must also be possible to achieve it. The dream is fed by those around us who seem to come closer to that dream of perfection than we are. They are seen as more perfect mothers or fathers than we are. Others are more perfect at a similar vocation than we are. Those impressions feed the hungry dream of our own perfection. The truth of the matter is that we can grow in our skills, in our understanding, in maturity of faith, but perfection is not achievable. That dream is real. The closest we come to purity is when we become an offering to God who receives our imperfection and declares it right and good.

■ ■ ■

Help us to grow, Lord, that we might present ourselves as an offering to you who can make all things right. Amen.

March 29

Psalm 22:27-28
All the ends of the earth shall remember and turn to the
Lord, and all the families of the nations bow before him. For
the kingship belongs to the Lord; he rules over the nations.

■ ■ ■

In my first year as a pastor, there was a week when I was having trouble writing a sermon. As much as I stared and studied the text, I couldn't think of a thing to say. I was concerned about how it would make me look. I was serving a small mission congregation. I decided to take a risk and tell them the truth instead of babbling during the sermon time. They appreciated my honesty. They found it a refreshing change of pace from any preacher they had ever known. They said, "Pastor, that was terrific! How courageous of you to tell us the truth! We loved it, but don't ever do that again." Pastors forget sometimes that we are servants of the Lord. I had to learn that the sermon was not about me, but about the proclamation of God's Good News to his beloved people. My own ego got in the way of the Word that the people themselves were hungry to hear and expected from me. It was a tough lesson but an important one to recognize that God is God and we can think better on our knees.

■ ■ ■

Holy God, forgive us when we forget to worship you. Amen.

March 30

Romans 4:20-22
No distrust made Abraham waver concerning the promise
of God, but he grew strong in his faith as he gave glory to
God, being fully convinced that God was able to do what he
had promised. Therefore his faith "was reckoned to him as
righteousness."

■ ■ ■

Recently, while clearing out some files, I ran across the evaluation I received from my seminary professors. I had been startled by two words and I was even more startled when I read them again so many years later. It said, "Strong faith." I didn't know what they saw back then, but I know my faith is light years beyond what it was. Daily I am reminded of how much stronger it needs to be and stand in awe of the witness of faithful giants around me. Faith truly is a gift given to us so that we might have a relationship with God. It is not our own doing, but it is God working through us for others. Sometimes I think our job is just to keeping our faith fertilized. God will strengthen it.

■ ■ ■

Precious Lord, strengthen our faith so that we might be a blessing to others. Amen.

March 31

Mark 8:31-33
Jesus began to teach them that the Son of Man must undergo great suffering, and be rejected by the elders, the chief priests, and the scribes, and be killed, and after three days rise again. He said all this quite openly. And Peter took him aside and began to rebuke him. But turning and looking at his disciples, he rebuked Peter and said, "Get behind me, Satan! For you are setting your mind not on divine things but on human things."

■ ■ ■

Jesus basically says, "I've got bad news and good news." Not only that, Jesus took on all the bad news and became the best news. Suffering and death is the bad news. Rising again is the incredibly wonderful news. All Peter hears is the bad news. He doesn't even take a breath over the rising before he is again stepping on Jesus about the suffering and death. We have a tendency of doing that. We focus on the glass half-empty. To hover at the cross and miss Easter is to live like fools. I have had my foolish moments. Blessings are those people in our lives who vibrate with the Good News so much that we can't help but feel the beat.

■ ■ ■

Lord, rise into our day with your love and grace and if necessary, Lord, hit us over the head with it. Amen.

April 1

Mark 10:9
Therefore what God has joined together, let no one
separate.

■ ■ ■

Science tells us that the second law of thermodynamics is that all matter tends to move to its lowest form of energy. A wooden chair will eventually disintegrate. A car will eventually become rust. The physical forces of the universe seem to be at work in our relationships as well. Without work put into it, we become separated from our God, our loved ones, and ourselves. To stay together requires energy, often more energy than a human being can muster. By the cross of Christ, we know that God is well aware of the forces which drive us from each other and separate us from our best selves. A new power unleashed in the world is one which flies in the face of the forces of sin. God is creating a new thing.

■ ■ ■

Lord God, help us to embrace the power of the cross that we might all be one in Christ. Amen.

April 2

Numbers 21:7-8
The people came to Moses and said, "We have sinned by speaking against the Lord and against you; pray to the Lord to take away the serpents from us." So Moses prayed for the people. And the Lord said to Moses, "Make a poisonous serpent, and set it on a pole; and everyone who is bitten shall look at it and live."

■ ■ ■

As stories go, I have to admit this is a weird one. In our more sophisticated society, we raise a skeptical eyebrow to such primitive tales and toss them into the fires of irrelevancy. The truth of God's Word would still burn in the firelight and find its way into the world as truth always finds a way. Beyond a metal snake and a pole, this is a story about a God who is creating a relationship with his people, requires loyalty, encourages conversation, and promotes trust and faith. There is healing and hope and the restoration of life for those who believe. We are a people who look at these strange stories through the filter of an Easter promise. We who look at a man suffering and dying on a cross and believe that through that cross there is life. In the time of Moses, God was getting humanity ready for faith in the one who would and could save them.

■ ■ ■

Stir in us, O Lord, the faith that we need to believe in your promises and trust in your mercy. Amen.

April 3

Psalm 19:14
Let the words of my mouth and the meditation of my heart
be acceptable to you, O Lord, my rock and my redeemer.

■ ■ ■

All pastors start their sermons a bit differently. Some say a prayer....some give a greeting to the congregation....some just dive right in. I have known many who use this prayer before they begin to preach. I have prayed this prayer thousands of times, but it is usually when I am talking privately with a person. There is nothing more humbling than to be allowed into the intimate thoughts of people struggling with the deepest problems and their most precious relationships. On our own, we are more than likely to blurt out the wrong thing or focus on the wrong piece of information. Living a life of constant prayer includes those moments when we are listening to one another and are afraid that we don't know what to say. This ancient prayer is an open-handed offering - asking God to take our humble, flawed, misguided words and thoughts and make them into a blessing. God can and God will do just that.

■ ■ ■

Let the words of my mouth and the meditation of my heart be acceptable to you, O Lord, my rock and my redeemer. Amen.

94

April 4

Ephesians 2:4-5
But God, who is rich in mercy, out of the great love with
which he loved us even when we were dead through our
trespasses, made us alive together with Christ - by grace
you have been saved

■ ■ ■

I heard the comment from a person whose job environment had become impossibly difficult and whose health was sapping her energy. She said, "Can I call in dead today?" We can, in a sense, call in dead. By confessing our sin, we admit we are dead. Martin Luther taught that we should also remember our baptism every day when we wash our faces in the morning. To remember our baptism is to remember that we die with Christ and are raised again with him to new life. We experience little Easters when we face the difficulties with hope. We live those Easters by offering good works, not as a way to earn points with God, but as a way to give thanks. God receives all the messages of those who call in dead and meets them where they are with love, grace, and eternal life.

■ ■ ■

Amazing Grace, how sweet the sound that saved a wretch like me. Amen.

April 5

John 3:20-21
For all who do evil hate the light and do not come to
the light, so that their deeds may not be exposed. But
those who do what is true come to the light, so that it
may be clearly seen that their deeds have been done in
God.

■ ■ ■

Research has told us what we have often suspected that
light plays a factor in our mental well-being. When I first
moved to Ohio to attend seminary, it was literally 6 months
before I saw a cloudless, sunny day. The clouds left me
feeling unsettled, solemn, morose. Even though all the
other circumstances of my life remained the same, a few
days of sunshine altered my perspective. Sinful behavior
tends to make us skulk around in the shadows. We use the
cover of darkness to whisper ill will or damage reputations
or use other people. After a while, all that darkness just
breeds more darkness. To walk in the light as children of
God is to have our sinfulness exposed. The light becomes
the sources of great discomfort but the only path to healing.

■ ■ ■

Help us today to choose to walk in the light, in the name of
Christ. Amen.

April 6

Mark 10:49
Jesus stood still and said, "Call him here." And they called the blind man, saying to him, "Take heart; get up, he is calling you. "

■ ■ ■

Jesus had built momentum as he was moving head-long toward Jerusalem where his great battle would be joined. His following was a large, noisy entourage moving with excitement. The air was filled with the din of anticipation, murmuring travelers, and the constant daily cries of beggars. It is not a scene unfamiliar to us since most of our days are full of busy-ness. Perhaps even more subtle and sublime than the verse "Jesus wept" is the verse "Jesus stood still." A moment's hesitation was a luxury he could not afford. He would have a moment alone in a garden later, but now there was still ground to cover. Christ's ability to be so in tune with the voice of a single beggar is a great wonder. Every step toward the cross was one of compassion. Compassion extended one person at a time until he finally took on the world.

■ ■ ■

Lord, teach us to stand still and listen for your voice. Amen.

97

April 7

Jeremiah 31:33-34
But this is the covenant that I will make with the house of
Israel after those days, says the Lord: I will put my law
within them, and I will write it on their hearts; and I will
be their God, and they shall be my people. No longer shall
they teach one another, or say to each other, "Know the
Lord," for they shall all know me, from the least of them to
the greatest, says the Lord; for I will forgive their iniquity,
and remember their sin no more.

■ ■ ■

The more I have travel the better I have become at packing
my luggage. One great lesson I picked up along the way is
to lay out my clothes and then eliminate at least of quarter
of them. I always tend to carry too much. Between the cost
of checking our luggage and our distrust of the airlines to
handle it, we "carry on" more often. We carry on other kinds
of baggage in our lives. We carry grudges because it is less
work than grace and forgiveness. God agrees to take on the
heavy luggage of a relationship with people who don't know
how to pack. It is time to take a look at what we have been
lugging around and time to let go of the unnecessary
baggage. It is time to remember the God who is lugging us
around.

■ ■ ■

Holy God, you hold us in the palm of your hand. Teach
us to lighten the load learning to forgive. Amen.

April 8

Psalm 51:11-12
Do not cast me away from your presence, and do not take
your holy spirit from me. Restore to me the joy of your
salvation, and sustain in me a willing spirit. Then I will
teach transgressors your ways, and sinners will return to
you.

■ ■ ■

An old folk song running through my head, "When we will
ever learn...when will we ever learn...." When will we learn
that our lives are not about being perfect. It is not about
living up to expectations. It is not about being right - it is
not about our dreams. It is not about being happy. King
David knew. Apostle Paul knew. And in our heart of hearts
thanks to the Spirit of God we know the truth. The truth is
that it is not about being perfect. It is about being forgiven.
We are lost and hopeless without it.

■ ■ ■

When will we ever learn....Lord...when will we ever learn?
According to your steadfast love, don't give up on us. Amen.

April 9

Hebrews 5:8-9
Although he was a Son, he learned obedience through what
he suffered; and having been made perfect, he became the
source of eternal salvation for all who obey him.

■ ■ ■

Anyone who tries to convince us that the Christian life is
supposed to be smooth sailing, no difficulties, easy answers
and constant contentment is telling us lies. There is no
doubt we long to believe it. We want to know that there is
something that either we can do or can be offered to us to
take away our suffering and leave us in peace. In the midst
of our angst and pain, we consider Jesus submissive and
obedient to the will of God to the point of tears. Somehow,
knowing his suffering makes me forget my own. Maybe that
is the point.

■ ■ ■

Precious Lord, teach us to pray, and cry and give up our
lives for one another as you have done for us. Amen.

April 10

John 12:21,24
They came to Philip, who was from Bethsaida in Galilee,
and said to him, "Sir, we wish to see Jesus." Philip went
and told Andrew; then Andrew and Philip went and told
Jesus. Very truly, I tell you, unless a grain of wheat falls
into the earth and dies, it remains just a single grain; but if
it dies, it bears much fruit.

■ ■ ■

I often like to ask people, "Where have you seen Jesus recently?" The responses are full of wonderful events, joyous moments, beautiful displays of creation, tender conversations. When they asked to see Jesus, Jesus talked about death. If we want to see Jesus, we need to look at death. Everything that Jesus has to offer us comes through the reality of death. We bear in us the condemnation of our sin and we will die. Jesus bore our sin and he died. If we want to see Jesus, we must see the death of a man who didn't deserve to die. It is in his dying that something new is created and offered to us.

■ ■ ■

Lord God, make yourself known to us. Amen.

April 11

Acts 2: 38-40
Peter said to them, "Repent, and be baptized every one of you in the name of Jesus Christ so that your sins may be forgiven; and you will receive the gift of the Holy Spirit. For the promise is for you, for your children, and for all who are far away, everyone whom the Lord our God calls to him."

■ ■ ■

There is a story about a little boy who had no one with whom to play and asked his mother to play darts with him. She felt for him and agreed and asked him if he wanted her to throw all her darts first and then he could throw all his darts or should they take turns. He shook his head and said, "I want to throw ALL the darts!" Then the mother replied, "Then what I am suppose I do?" He said, "You stand there and say 'Wonderful!'" Exhortation is the gift of encouragement. Sometimes we need encouragement to confess our sins, to do the right thing, to put one foot in front of the other each day. We may wither without it.....with it, we become who God intended us to be. We are in this together -let us exhort one another.

■ ■ ■

Lord God, make us aware this day of those who need the encouragement that we can freely give. Amen.

April 12

Psalm 116:3-4
The cords of death entangled me; the grip of the grave took hold of me; I came to grief and sorrow. Then I called upon the name of the Lord: "O Lord, I pray you, save my life."

■ ■ ■

It doesn't take life-threatening circumstances to make us feel tangled up in details and strangled by constraints of time. We struggle against the ropes and knots of our situation until we come to the conclusion that we need help. Often our heads are so muddled we don't even know how or who to ask especially when those around us have their own web of knots to untied. There is something powerful in finally resting inside our tangled lives and just saying, "Lord, help me" knowing that the words are free to find their way to the one who listens and cares.

■ ■ ■

Lord our hands are tied by time and filled with things to do. Help us breath and gently claim our Easter freedom to ask for help. Amen.

April 13

I Peter 1:21-22
Through him you have come to trust in God, who raised him from the dead and gave him glory, so that your faith and hope are set on God. Now that you have purified your souls by your obedience to the truth so that you have genuine mutual love, love one another deeply from the heart.

■ ■ ■

We trust God because he gives us Easter. Because of Easter we can choose to turn from our self-serving ways and turn our lives inside out for others. That is what genuine love feels like sometimes....like we are turning ourselves inside out. Love is stretching and risking the fabric of our hearts. It is giving our best selves and sacrificing our soul's safety. Love exposes us but compels us to keep risking because it is just so right. It is a little cross, a little suffering, a little Christ. But because of God's big Easter, we are free to choose to be obedient to what love requires time after time.

■ ■ ■

Turn me inside out, Holy God, that I may be the arms to embrace those who have not known Easter yet this day. Amen.

April 14

Luke 24:18-19
Then one of them, whose name was Cleopas, answered him,
"Are you the only stranger in Jerusalem who does not know
the things that have taken place there in these days?" He
asked them, "What things?" They replied, "The things about
Jesus of Nazareth, who was a prophet mighty in deed and
word before God and all the people."

■ ■ ■

The rabbinic style of teaching is one which uses a question
and answer format rather than long lectures. The teacher
expects the students to have done their reading and know
the information. The Q&A process helps a student integrate
the information, so that it becomes a part of who they are.
Jesus was a good rabbi.....always asking good questions
which helped people talk about what was on their minds.
His questions helped them think about things they needed
to think about. Jesus continues to ask us the most
important question of them all...."Who do you say that I
am?"

■ ■ ■

Lord Jesus, walk with us and ask us the important
questions so that we will hear our faith alive in the answers
for ourselves and others. Amen.

April 15

Acts 2:46-47
Day by day, as they spent much time together in the
temple, they broke bread at home and ate their food with
glad and generous hearts, praising God and having the
goodwill of all the people. And day by day the Lord added to
their number those who were being saved.

■ ■ ■

"Day by day, dear Lord three things I pray: to see thee more
clearly, to love thee more dearly, follow thee more nearly."
This simple prayer has been sung in a 60's musical, used
frequently by the founding monk of the Jesuit order in
1534, and written by Sir Richard of Chichester in 1275. Day
by day is the pace of our lives of faith. In the daily acts of
spending time with one another, sharing a meal, giving our
selves, praising God and praying for one another we
nurture one another's relationship with God. God blesses
our daily acts of mercy and grace by giving our hearts the
capacity to widen our circle and welcome more sisters and
brothers to the feast.

■ ■ ■

Today, Lord, we have a thousand things to do and doing
them with you makes it splendid. Amen.

April 16

Psalm 133:1
How very good and pleasant it is when kindred live
together in unity!

■ ■ ■

At a gathering of college students, we discussed the Easter story and what we liked the most about their Easter worship experiences at home. I teased one of the students because all he talked about was the food and time with his family. I said, "But what about Jesus rising from the dead!" And he said, "Oh that's a given!" The students truly do love their families, and often speak of cherished time with grandparents and other loved ones. The joy of Easter is not isolated in one place but lives in the luxury of food, the grace of families, and a peaceful gathers. The gift of Easter, though not to be taken for granted, is still a miracle in that it is, in fact, "a given."

■ ■ ■

Risen Lord, may we find the joy of Easter in the company of those who love us and in learning to love others beyond ourselves. Amen.

April 17

I Peter 2:24-25
He himself bore our sins in his body on the cross, so that,
free from sins, we might live for righteousness; by his
wounds you have been healed. For you were going astray
like sheep, but now you have returned to the shepherd and
guardian of your souls.

■ ■ ■

One Christmas, I was given a wooden nativity set that had
the baby Jesus resting not in a manger but carved in his
mother's arms. I was told by the giver that it was so I would
never have to worry about losing him. The favorite image of
Jesus I have in my heart is as a shepherd holding a sheep
in his arms. It reminds me that I never have to worry about
losing myself. He finds us when we are lost. He takes us as
we are. He bears our burdens and holds us close. Just at the
moment when we think we are crawling around alone in
the world, we hear God's heart beat and find ourselves
fussing inside his wounded arms.

■ ■ ■

Precious Savior, thank you for your faithfulness and love.
Help us to open our arms to others. Amen.

April 18

John 10:9-10
I am the gate. Whoever enters by me will be saved, and will come in and go out and find pasture. The thief comes only to steal and kill and destroy. I came that they may have life, and have it abundantly.

■ ■ ■

Abundant life on any given day means something different. For one person it may mean the freedom to spend money without worrying about cash flow. For another it may be the richness of family relationships. For still another it may be the opportunity to have stimulating experiences or meaningful work. We blaze ahead to define and reach for whatever "abundant" means to us. We have a tendency to take for granted the "life" part. Jesus came that we may have life. We get to play around in this thing called life because he made sure we had it to play with. We don't have to steal what has been freely given.

■ ■ ■

Lord God, help us this day to describe our lives as abundant simply and thankfully because you gave it to us. Amen.

April 19

Psalm 31:5,15-16
Into your hands I commend my spirit, for you have
redeemed me, O Lord, O God of truth. My times are in your
hand; rescue me from the hand of my enemies, and from
those who persecute me. Make your face to shine upon your
servant, and in your loving kindness save me.

■ ■ ■

I have been taught from my youth to stand on my own two feet, to be independent and self-sufficient. The phrase "I need help" was not one that was encouraged to be uttered. Yet who among us has not, in fact, reached out for a hand to steady us or shot a desperate prayer into the night air? In the compassionate balance of God's family, we need the freedom to express our need for help. We also need to have someone who can listen to our cry and respond to what we need. Our Lord receives our prayers and stirs up the resources of the heart of his people. At any given time we are the ones in need or the ones being stirred to help.

■ ■ ■

Lord God, give us the courage to tell you what we need and even more courage to give to those in need. Amen.

April 20

I Peter 2: 9-10
But you are a chosen race, a royal priesthood, a holy nation,
God's own people, in order that you may proclaim the
mighty acts of him who called you out of darkness in to his
Marvelous light. Once you were not a people, but now you
are God's people; once you had not received mercy, but now
you have received mercy.

■ ■ ■

Our innate need to belong appears in our sub-conscience as a dream...a deep and pleasant longing or a phantom pain of something we once had. We want to know that we are a part of something greater than ourselves, that our lives have meaning, and that we are profoundly woven into the fabric of those we love. In the promise of our God, we are given the gift of belonging, of being claimed for no other reason than God's delight. In a single promise, we have home, family, freedom and a reason to get up in the morning.

■ ■ ■

Holy God, we are in awe of your creative word that continues to make things happens. At your word, we are healed, loved, forgiven, adopted and set free to serve. Keep up the good word, Lord. Amen.

April 21

John 14:2-3
In my Father's house there are many dwelling places. If it were not so, would I have told you that I go to prepare a place for you? And if I go and prepare a place for you, I will come again and will take you to myself, so that where I am, there you may be also.

■ ■ ■

After spending anytime house shopping, square footage gets to be a big issue. My first instinct when hearing about God's house was to speculate about the square footage and the floor plan. Buying and moving into a new house gives one a new appreciation for what goes into turning empty rooms into living places. Human beings have always been curious about what heaven might look like. Here we are told all that we truly need to know. We don't know about square footage or decor, all that we know for certain is that our name is on the door, that we will belong there, and Jesus will be there too. It just doesn't get any better than that.

■ ■ ■

Holy God, may we appreciate today the real estate in which we find ourselves. Help us to find peace in the promise of your open door. Amen.

April 22

Psalm 66: 16, 20
Come and hear, all you who fear God, and I will tell what
he has done for me. Blessed be God, because he has not
rejected my prayer or removed his steadfast love from me.

■ ■ ■

I have yet to meet a person who has said that they are
completely satisfied with their prayer life. We all continue
to hunger to learn and grow in our conversations with God.
The avenues, the methods, the reminders, the tools are
numerous and all roads lead to the presence of the Lord
which is always a great place to be. Even in our most beat-
up moments or times of shame, the Lord offers us his ear,
his mercy, and his love. To know that we are heard,
understood, forgiven, and loved by the Living God is a cause
for hope and praise.

■ ■ ■

Lord God, thank you for being constantly within earshot so
that we can know the magnitude of your grace. Amen.

April 23

John 14:18-19
I will not leave you orphaned; I am coming to you. In a little
while the world will no longer see me, but you will see me;
because I live, you also will live.

■ ■ ■

No matter our age, we feel the thunder in our soul when we lose a parent. We have moments where our orphanhood seems to lay across our shoulders. Parents are those people on the front lines of our lives. They help us to recognize love when we see and feel it. For some it may mean hearing the words, for others it may mean chicken soup or a hug or a ride to the doctor's. Love makes itself known in powerful ways in our lives so that we are not orphaned. Love makes us aware of the living Christ at work around us and through us. If Christ is so alive with his love in others, then Christ is just as alive and willing to move through us....so that no one is orphaned.

■ ■ ■

Lord God, we are not alone in you. Help us to spread the word. Amen.

April 24

Isaiah 50:4
The Lord God has given me the tongue of a teacher, that I
may know how to sustain the weary with a word. Morning
by morning he wakens - wakens my ear to listen to those
who are taught.

■ ■ ■

I have had the privilege of working with some great teachers and colleagues. The best of the best were those who taught by example. One dear colleague I had could easily "sustain the weary with a word" but even more importantly, he was a teacher who listened. One of his pastoral mentors taught him always to "listen to the sergeants" - in other words, pay close attention to the voices of valued leaders who were in the trenches and the frontlines of discipleship. When Jesus taught, crowds gathered to hear his words and were lifted up by his teaching. Jesus listened to the voices of the sick, the lonely, the sinners.

■ ■ ■

Lord God, in the blessedness of our relationships with you and one another, help us to be open to your teaching and grateful every day for your listening ear. Amen.

April 25

Psalm 31:13-14
For I hear the whispering of many—terror all around!—as they scheme together against me, as they plot to take my life. But I trust in you, O LORD; I say, 'You are my God.'

■ ■ ■

In conversations with young adults who are often at the beginning of relationships headed toward marriage, I often have asked them when they think marriage actually starts. Some say at their engagement, others on the wedding day, still others say when the paper is signed. Many will speak of a time unique to them as a couple. Nevertheless, the vows which say "You are my husband and you are my wife" spoken out loud to one another in the company of witnesses is a powerful moment. It is one of many defining moments in a marriage. So also, in our relationship with God, we have some defining moments in which, despite what is going on around us, we declare who we are. We are God's servants and we are greatly loved.

■ ■ ■

Lord God, may we define ourselves this day as completely loved by you. Amen.

April 26

Philippians 2:6-7
Though he was in the form of God, did not regard equality
with God as something to be exploited, but emptied himself,
taking the form of a slave, being born in human likeness.

■　■　■

If anyone could have claimed to have rights, privilege, and entitlement, it was Jesus. It doesn't take human beings long to start claiming our rights. As children, we start early expecting privileges. We believe we deserve to have the new toy, to watch the television, to play with friends, to own those jeans, to borrow the car, to put our younger siblings in their place. We believe we deserve the raise, the recognition from colleagues, the attention of family. Jesus offers us a different way to be human - humble service, obedience, and sacrifice. One way of life fixes us, forever, in the selfishness of childhood. The other helps us to grow up into a lifestyle of service.

■　■　■

Lord God, help us to choose to be the best of who you created us to be. Amen.

April 27

Mark 9:42
*If any of you put a stumbling block before one of these little
ones who believe in me, it would be better for you if a great
millstone were hung around your neck and you were
thrown into the sea.*

■ ■ ■

When we were children, my siblings and I would play in the
living room. We were often oblivious to the fact that we
were strolling in front of the television that my father was
trying to watch. We would hear him say in a calm voice
without a hint of anger, "You make a better door than you
do a window." It always took us a few seconds to
understand that he could not see through us and we should
get out of the way. We can't be God for anyone, but we can
clear the way for someone to see the Christ who loves,
forgives and redeems. It is disturbing to realize that our
words and actions might pose obstacles for someone's faith.
Our most sincere efforts to help can be muddied by our need
to control. We make a significant step of growth when we
recognize that we may be a part of the problem rather than
the solution. Grace and forgiveness are the hinges on which
we can swing to stay connected and humbly get out of the
way.

■ ■ ■

Lord, grant us the wisdom to know when to help and when
to get out of the way. Amen.

April 28

Mark 10:27
Jesus looked at them and said, "For mortals it is
impossible, but not for God; for God all things are possible.

■ ■ ■

I am a big picture person. I tend to see the little dramas in the context of a much larger one. To look alone at the rich, young ruler's conversation with Christ is to be struck with the heartfelt attempt of a person to find salvation and eternal life. Even more so we are stunned by the harsh totality of Jesus' words: "Sell everything." This seeker walks away struggling with what it means to be rich and poor. To find the big picture, we draw back the camera lens on this scene and see disciples who are listening. They ask the questions of Jesus on our behalf. How is it possible for anyone to be saved when the criteria seemed completely out of human reach? The fact is that salvation is out of human reach. It is not something that a ruler can buy or disciple can perform. How God's people are saved is a huge miracle but the even bigger miracle is that God wants to save us.

■ ■ ■

Lord God, thank for giving us the big picture of your grace and mercy. Amen.

April 29

Ezekiel 37:27
My dwelling place shall be with them; and I will be their
God, and they shall be my people.

■ ■ ■

The history of the people of God from ancient times to the present has been one of scattering and gathering. The scattering happened often after a united people behaved as if they no longer needed God. During the time of their scattering, they developed a new appreciation of what they had and who they were as God's people. They rekindled a deep longing for home. Repeatedly, God gathered his scattered people. Though the times of dispersal were challenging, they were never forgotten by God. God always had their forwarding address. And when the time was right, God called them to gather again. God called the people home. In our scattered condition on the earth, we know what it is too long for home and to be one with each other and our God. It is a longing that gives us a glimpse of God's heart.

■ ■ ■

Lord God, we, your scattered people, listen to your gathering cry and long for home. Amen.

April 30

Ezekiel 45:3
In the holy district you shall measure off a section...in
which shall be the sanctuary, the most holy place.

■ ■ ■

The poet T.S. Eliot spoke of love, and ultimately God as being the "still point of the turning world." When so little ever stays the same, when the children grow before our eyes, when the gods of busy schedules are thrown their daily sacrifices of our time, we need no reminder of a turning world. We do, however, need to find those places that hold the still and unchanging truth of who we are and who God is. The temple for the people of Israel was that irrefutable place to which they could go, at least could dream they could go, and know, beyond a doubt, that God was present. Holy spaces are where the walls between the Kingdom here and the Kingdom not yet are so thin that one can almost see through them. It is where we can glimpse the peaceful presence of God and where we can dare to press our palms on the fortress and feel a heart beating. With the gift of the Holy Spirit, Christ gave us the ability to make any space holy, any point in a turning world still, any wall, a window even if only for a moment.

■ ■ ■

Lord God, grant us a quiet stillness in the constant turbulence of our days. Amen.

121

May 1

2 Kings 2:1-2
Now when the Lord was about to take Elijah up to heaven
by a whirlwind, Elijah and Elisha were on their way from
Gilgal. Elijah said to Elisha, "Stay here; for the Lord has
sent me as far as Bethel." But Elisha said, "As the Lord
lives, and as you yourself live, I will not leave you." So they
went down to Bethel.

■ ■ ■

When community is created by the Holy Spirit, there is a
transfusion that happens between people. The spirit pulses
through the veins of the soul from one person to another
like an IV transferring blood. We can't make the flow
happen but we can keep the lines open and resist behavior
that would try to block its path. Together we can be more
than the sum of who we are individually because of the
dynamic nature of God's spirit in us. God blesses us with
friends, family, community, neighbors, and co-workers to be
the vehicles for that spirit. The journey is a blessed one
when we walk together in the presence of God.

■ ■ ■

Holy God, send your spirit into our conversations that we
might infuse one another with your life-giving will. Amen.

May 2

Philippians 1:3-5
I thank my God every time I remember you, constantly praying with joy in every one of my prayers for all of you, because of your sharing in the gospel from the first day until now.

■ ■ ■

The letters of Paul were written on scrolls and carried by messengers. They were cherished, re-read, and became a part of the canon of scriptures that contain the Word of God. It is hard to imagine any of our correspondence today being cherished, read, re-read, copied, saved, believed to be divinely inspired, and shared with others. I have a friend who knows how important words are to me and often sends me cards or notes - for thanks, encouragement, or celebrations. I read them more than once and I have saved most of them. If we knew that our words would live beyond us, if we knew that the words we say, post, and text would be eternal testimonies of our loves and life, would we take more care? I would pray that the plethora of my words that are silly and selfish would be forgiven and that the ones that speak of Jesus would be believed

■ ■ ■

O Lord, may my thoughts and words be acceptable to you, and worth repeating. Amen.

May 3

John 2:11
Very truly, I tell you, we speak of what we know and testify to what we have seen.

■ ■ ■

There was an article in a sports magazine about a famous football player who made a dramatic comeback after a long, dark time of drug abuse and bad behavior. The player pointed to Christ as being the person who turned his life around. The sports writer had seen this story before and took a critical approach to his interview with the player and the investigation into his life past and present. At the end, the writer admitted that even though one may doubt that Christ had anything to do with this football player, it is difficult to refute the testimony of a changed life. I have seen lives changed through hope, prayer, healing, and forgiveness. I have been changed by the daily reminders of God's grace in my life. Those who are most to be pitied are those who have known grace and seem unable to extend it to others. We speak of what we have seen and heard. It is difficult to refute the testimony of a changed life.

■ ■ ■

Holy God, help us to hear and believe those whose lives are changed by your love. Amen.

May 4

Psalm 23:1-3
The Lord is my shepherd; I shall not be in want. He makes
me lie down in green pastures and leads me beside still
waters. He revives my soul and guides me along right
pathways for his name's sake.

■　■　■

My first surprise when I arrived in Texas to live and work
was a typical reaction for newcomers to the state. It is
greener than I expected. (At least parts of it are!) The Texas
spring is its most gentle season. The air is refreshingly cool.
The sun has a soft touch. The bluebonnets make their
appearance if only briefly. It doesn't take much to revive us
from the gray days of winter or brace us for the blistering
days of summer. The dark and difficult times happen in the
rhythm of our lives, but God provides places to rest. A walk
in the sun, a beer with a friend, a conversation with a child,
have power to remind us of God's refreshing and life-giving
spirit.

■　■　■

Open the eyes of our hearts, Lord, so that we can see the
drink of refreshing grace you are constantly extending to
us. Amen.

May 5

I John 1:8-9
If we say that we have no sin, we deceive ourselves, and the truth is not in us. If we confess our sins, he who is faithful and just will forgive us our sins and cleanse us from all unrighteousness.

■ ■ ■

These words are a part of our church's liturgy for confession and forgiveness. I remember when I first heard those words spoken in worship many years ago. It was breathtakingly honest. To begin worship declaring that we are sinners and that denial is not an option was a bold way to get people's attention. We cherish honesty and we expect it from others. We can't function very well if we are operating on false information. Our relationship with God requires no less honesty. God offers us his love, grace, and mercy and it is quickly delivered in the words of forgiveness to a sinner with an honest and contrite heart.

■ ■ ■

Forgive us, Lord, for we have sinned against you in thought, word and deed. Amen.

126

May 6

John 20:30-31
Now Jesus did many other signs in the presence of the
disciples, which are not written in this book. But these are
written so that you may come to believe that Jesus is the
Messiah, the Son of God, and that through believing you
may have life in his name.

■ ■ ■

My seminary professor asked us for the single greatest
piece of evidence that convinces us that the resurrection is
true. It was difficult to pick just one. Thomas saying "My
Lord, and My God" after his own doubt has always been
huge in my heart and mind. His doubt spoke for us all and
his words of conviction witnessed to us all. The other piece
of evidence is the history of the faithful followers since that
first small band of disciples were gathered. The testimony
of the witnesses to the resurrection lit the flame for us all
today. Despite heresies, misguided leaders, controversies
about scriptures, there is a blissfully simple and profound
witness to one single person saying, "I know that my
Redeemer lives."

■ ■ ■

May we be today a part of the great legacy of witnesses to
the resurrection. Amen.

May 7

Matthew 21:32
Even after you saw it, you did not change your minds and
believe him.

■ ■ ■

In the life of faith, there are always those days laced with doubt. It is as if your soul was hacked by a computer virus that infects just enough to crash the whole system. We need something outside ourselves to cleanse our program, to restore our faith. We need to see with our own eyes. Even those who witnessed Jesus' signs and heard him speak, still had trouble at times believing. When my faith falters, it is strengthened by what I can see and feel - works of mercy and touches of compassion. But faith is not created by convincing evidence. It is a new way of living, of stepping out into the world, of looking at one's community, family, and friends. Faith is to change from the inside out and brave a new way of believing about ourselves and the world. In that way, those who walked with Jesus have no advantage. We all must learn to walk inside out.

■ ■ ■

Lord God, I believe. Help my unbelief. Amen.

May 8

Acts 3:19
Repent therefore, and turn to God so that your sins may be wiped out.

■ ■ ■

Anyone saying "Repent!" conjures up images of some crazed person on a street corner screaming to passers-by. Public plazas and college campuses tend to be magnets for wandering street preachers who take to the public arenas to vent their spiritual spleens. We intentionally turn off the volume to such reminders because we don't trust the messenger. We all need people in our lives that hold us accountable and call us to become the person God meant us to be. Our relationships are a gift from God to challenge us to lives of deeper love and greater faith. When we are called to repentance for the sake of love, we listen.

■ ■ ■

Holy God, help us to hear the call to repentance with openness and hope. In the name of Christ, Amen.

May 9

Psalm 4:4-5
When you are disturbed, do not sin; ponder it on your beds,
and be silent. Offer right sacrifices, and put your trust in
the LORD.

■ ■ ■

I shared a room with my sister growing up. Through the
turbulence of adolescence and teenage years, I so wanted
my privacy in order to feel free to be weak. I learned how to
cry silently as the tears fall into ears and the intake of a
breath is intentionally controlled. Over the years, the
release of tears after a stressful day became less worrisome
events and the beginning of prayer. Sleep comes as we pull
our confidence in God's love and grace under our damp
chins and trust.

■ ■ ■

O Lord, hear our prayers, be patient with our tears, forgive
us and help us enjoy the grace of each new day. Amen.

May 10

I John 3:1-2
See what love the Father has given us, that we should be
called children of God; and that is what we are. The reason
the world does not know us is that it did not know him.
beloved, we are God's children now; what we will be has not
yet been revealed. What we do know is this: when he is
revealed, we will be like him, for we will see him as he is.

■ ■ ■

There are few feelings more unsettling than not being
understood especially by those we care about. No one knows
us completely or can see completely into our motives, our
hearts. Even we are clouded in our own view of ourselves
and may not comprehend the complicated aspects of our
own fears and needs. As children of God, we know not only
that our Redeemer lives but that he lives in us. Our
understanding of who we are to God and a part of God's
nature himself is imbedded within us. We are not finished.
We are still on our way.

■ ■ ■

Holy God, may we be gentle with ourselves and one another
as we seek to be understood and to understand. Amen.

May 11

Luke 24:32
They said to each other, "Were not our hearts burning
within us while he was talking to us on the road, while he
was opening the scriptures to us?"

■ ■ ■

The first disciples had memorized the ancient texts and
prayers as young children and had found some degree of
comfort in the mystery of the words and the familiar
sounds. But it wasn't until the Risen Lord walked with
them on the road and ate with them that the scriptures
started to course through their veins and deliver God's life-
giving word. Time after time I have seen the experience of
the disciples on the Emmaus road repeat itself when people
gather to read the scriptures. The reading and discussing of
God's word with others on the faith journey with us is a life-
giving exercise.

■ ■ ■

Help us, Lord, to make the scriptures come alive for one
another. Amen.

May 12

Psalm 68:9-10
Rain in abundance, O God, you showered abroad; you
restored your heritage when it languished; your flock found
a dwelling in it; in your goodness, O God, you provided for
the needy.

■ ■ ■

Our journey of faith often is not a simple, even path meandering through a sweet meadow. It can be a slippery slope where two steps forward are truly met with more backward. Such it is in my own faith life when faced with unexpected obstacles, I rear back. I lose my footing and balance. I grope for a handhold. The blessing of a life of faith is that we have a history of handholds to remember. God consistently has been present with us. Handholds come to us in an assuring word or glance from a friend, in a sign like a rainbow or a butterfly, in the taste of bread and wine, in a splash of water or in the name of God's sweet son. Even as we journey, inside the heart of God we find rest and a glimpse of home.

■ ■ ■

Holy God, help us to remember your faithfulness to us in the past so that we can walk more peacefully through this wonderful day. Amen.

May 13

I Peter 5:5
In the same way, you who are younger must accept the
authority of the elders. And all of you must clothe
yourselves with humility in your dealings with one another,
for 'God opposes the proud, but gives grace to the humble.'

■ ■ ■

Unfortunately, power struggles between the old and the young have always been characteristic of that relationship. In my 50's I still bristle, at times, at the authority that those older have. I am also guilty of engaging poorly in the struggle for control with the young. But when God's wisdom shines, I love to listen to my elders and have met some children in my life that weaken my knees just to see the mountain of truth in their smiles. The blessed equalizer is God's hand guiding us all. When we embrace how God truly cares for us, the anxiety born of the struggle for power and control shows itself for what it is. It is something that can be cast aside, so that we can have more room to enjoy the generations which abound in our families and friends.

■ ■ ■

Lord God, help us to take pleasure in one another - both young and old. Amen.

May 14

Acts 2:3-4
Divided tongues, as of fire, appeared among them, and a
tongue rested on each of them. All of them were filled with
the Holy Spirit and began to speak in other languages, as
the Spirit gave them ability.

■ ■ ■

I think of Pentecost as the "Big Bang Theory" of the creation of the Church. It was an extraordinary moment that so inspired those present that the Christian faith spread throughout the world. I tried to illustrate a Pentecost sermon once by throwing a cherry bomb in a trash can. Fortunately we did not have to call the paramedics, but it was not one of my more well-thought-out sermon illustrations. God's illustration for us in Pentecost was far more brilliant. Our language is our tool for communication, but it is also a source of confusion. In a breath of wind and fire, God melted the confusion if only for a moment to show us all a vision of a world where we can be "together in one place" and completely at peace in the presence of the Lord.

■ ■ ■

Holy God, breathe your wind and fire on us so that we can speak with wisdom and clarity to the truth we have known in our lives. Amen.

135

May 15

Psalm 104:25-26

O Lord, how manifold are your works! In wisdom you have made them all; the earth is full of your creatures. Yonder is the great and wide sea with its living things too many to number, creatures both small and great.

■ ■ ■

I have been watching a nest of birds out my backdoor. The parents swoop in and out relentlessly feeding five demanding little mouths. I am amazed that with two parents coming and going independently of each other - each feeding one baby bird at a time - how do they know they are all getting fed equally? Even the nest is an engineering wonder. To look with fresh and attentive eyes to any single part of God's creation is also to discover the vast complexity of God's world and God's mind. That we get to enjoy this world is mind-boggling. That we were created in the image of God takes my breath away.

■ ■ ■

Make us attentive, O God, to the work of your mind and hands. Amen.

May 16

Corinthians 12:4-7
Now there are varieties of gifts, but the same Spirit;
and there are varieties of services, but the same Lord;
and there are varieties of activities, but it is the same God
who activates all of them in everyone. To each is given the
manifestation of the Spirit for the common good.

■ ■ ■

I once saw on the fireplace mantel of a person's home a
polished cross-section of a water pipe that had been
completely clogged with dirt and minerals. The man had
worked for the city repairing such pipes. In its polished
state, it was truly a unique work of art. It was also to me a
testimony to what we are called to be and how our sin
disrupts our calling. We were given gifts so that others
might receive God's blessings of grace, love, and mercy. We
are not the water but the water pipes. We benefit from the
grace of God that flows through us, but if we cling to it and
try to own it - the clogging begins. As the saying goes, love
isn't love until we give it away. It is a good thing to be God's
water pipe.

■ ■ ■

Holy God, pour into us your grace and truth. Use us as your
water way. Amen.

May 17

John 20:21-23
Jesus said to them again, "Peace be with you. As the Father
has sent me, so I send you." When he had said this, he
breathed on them and said to them, "Receive the Holy
Spirit. If you forgive the sins of any, they are forgiven them;
if you retain the sins of any, they are retained."

■ ■ ■

There is a small, often-forgotten portion of Luther's Small
Catechism called the "Office of the Keys." It is the authority
that all Christians have to forgive or not to forgive. In
essence, we hold the keys to forgiveness. A part of my
"leaving the house" choreography is that I check to see if I
have my purse, cell phones, and my keys. We wouldn't be
wise to leave without our keys. It is imprudent to walk into
our days without an understanding of the authority we
have to offer or not offer forgiveness to those who hurt or
offend us. God sent us as he sent Jesus into the world to
make it a place for grace.

■ ■ ■

Lord God, every time we grab our keys today help us to
remember that you open the door to your heart and the
Kingdom of Heaven for us. Amen.

May 18

Genesis 1:24-25
And God said, "Let the earth bring forth living creatures of
every kind: cattle and creeping things and wild animals of
the earth of every kind." And it was so. God made the wild
animals of the earth of every kind, and the cattle of every
kind, and everything that creeps upon the ground of every
kind. And God saw that it was good.

■　■　■

Zoologists would howl over the idea of all living creatures
being shoved into three categories: cattle, creeping things
and wild animals. Today there are hundreds of species
named and still undiscovered. But from the birth of the
earth and humanity, before we had words to name all the
critters, God called it good. In the beginning before we
messed things up royally, God called us good. The miracle
of the cross is that God still calls us good.

■　■　■

Holy God, thank you for creating and claiming us with your
good word. Help us to be someone's good word today. Amen.

139

May 19

Psalm 8:4-6
When I consider the heavens, the work of your fingers, the
moon and the stars you have set in their courses, what is
man that you should be mindful of him, the son of man that
you should seek him out? You have made him but little
lower than the angels; you adorn him with glory and honor;
you give him mastery over the works of your hands; you put
all things under his feet.

■ ■ ■

Despite my limited experience in world travel, I have seen
some spectacular scenery. Mountain vistas, prairies dressed
in velvet gold grass and ever-changing oceans. It commands
attention. It is almost impossible to take your eyes off it.
Surrounded by all the drama of our terrain, God chooses to
pay attention to us and seek us out. There is an
awkwardness to that kind of attention. It would be like
someone staring at us while we were in the Louvre staring
at the Mona Lisa. Somehow we don't think of ourselves as
masterpieces of a brilliant artist, but that we are. That we
are.

■ ■ ■

Master Designer, you do and continue to do great work!
Help us to understand how much you take pride in the
handiwork of our life so that we can honor it in all we do.
Amen.

May 20

2 Corinthians 13:13
The grace of the Lord Jesus Christ, the love of God, and the
communion of the Holy Spirit be with all of you.

■ ■ ■

These words are echoed in our worship liturgy. God has
given us these words through the disciples who first
witnessed the power of grace in Christ. With those words
we worship together and stand in the footprints of those
faithful ones. In our past, there are those who thought of us
and gave us the words of their witness. In our present we
have been given ones to love and forgive. In our future are
those who will remember our words, our faithful lives, our
witness to the truth. These words are the blessed handholds
for this, our peopled journey.

■ ■ ■

Holy God, Give us the words today to witness to what we
have seen and heard in our lives about the truth of Jesus
Christ. Amen.

May 21

Matthew 28:16-17
Now the eleven disciples went to Galilee to the mountain to which Jesus had directed them. When they saw him, they worshiped him; but some doubted.

■ ■ ■

"....but some doubted." That little phrase seems to leap off the page into our faces. Even after all they had witnessed, there were still doubts. Despite their doubts, they still lingered with the others. Strength in numbers, I suppose. Jesus does not stop and say, "Okay, let's spend some more time here clearing up these doubts you have." Jesus, instead, sends them into the world to make disciples, teach, and baptize. Oftentimes we cannot afford to be immobilized by our doubt. It is better to move with faith and carry our doubts with us, than to let our doubts bring us to a full stop. We couldn't have better reassurance than what Jesus offered his doubting disciples...."I am with you always."

■ ■ ■

Ease the burden of our doubt, Lord, with the movement of our faith toward those who need to hear that faith from us. Amen.

May 22

Deuteronomy 11:18
You shall put these words of mine in your heart and soul,
and you shall bind them as a sign on your hand, and fix
them as an emblem on your forehead.

■　■　■

I have a pet parrot named Reggie who talks or, more accurately, has the ability to repeat words he hears. Reggie tends to treat words like toys and he will repeat the ones he likes over and over and over again. As you can imagine, I have to be very careful talking around him because he might become enamored with words I don't particularly want to hear repeated constantly. It is not unlike an annoying song that runs through your head all day. But there are other words that cause me great delight whenever I hear them. We can choose to pick up and repeat the words of God so that those words leave an imprint on our lives. Today let's fall in love with God's word and bind it to our hands and hearts.

■　■　■

Holy God, speak to us that we may speak in the language of love, grace and mercy to those hungry to hear your word. Amen.

May 23

Psalm 31:22-24
Yet I said in my alarm, "I have been cut off from the sight of
your eyes. Nevertheless, you heard the sound of my
entreaty when I cried out to you. Love the Lord, all you who
worship him; the Lord protects the faithful, but repays to
the full those who act haughtily. Be strong and let your
heart take courage, all you who wait for the Lord.

■ ■ ■

There was a moment when I was walking in the mountains that I was aware of being very much alone...so alone that I began thinking that even my existence itself was a myth. Sometimes one's head waxes quite philosophical when in the woods. I decided to make a noise with my voice to confirm my own existence to myself. It was a mighty "Yaup" like the one taught by the Robin Williams' character in the movie Dead Poet's Society. In it, the teacher tells his students to yell as an expression of life. Prayer, when uttered in the dark, especially at the time when we feel the most alone, is a bold statement of faith. By whatever noise we utter in God's direction we testify that someone is listening. Even when we ourselves cannot find ourselves in the darkness, God can hear us as we cry, as we pray, as we "Yaup!"

■ ■ ■

Thank you, Lord, for listening for us and attending to our needful prayers. Amen.

144

May 24

Romans 1:16-17
I am not ashamed of the gospel; it is the power of God for
salvation to everyone who has faith, to the Jew first and
also to the Greek. For in it the righteousness of God is
revealed through faith for faith; as it is written, "The one
who is righteous will live by faith."

■ ■ ■

Through the ages, the Gospel has been mocked by
philosophers as foolishness. We, who identify ourselves to
be followers of Jesus, get defensive and invite the Gospel's
detractors into a courtroom of rational thought and
irrefutable evidence. We rarely convince anyone of the truth
through such sport. The opposite of being ashamed of the
Gospel is to embrace with pride the fact that it is truly
foolish. The only thing that we can boast about is not our
ability to earn God's grace and favor, but that we all have a
God who gives us grace and favor.

■ ■ ■

Gracious God, order our days and our deeds so that our
lives will reflect your love and grace. Amen.

May 25

Matthew 7:21-23
"Not everyone who says to me, 'Lord, Lord,' will enter the kingdom of heaven, but only the one who does the will of my Father in heaven. On that day many will say to me, 'Lord, Lord, did we not prophesy in your name, and do many deeds of power in your name?' Then I will declare to them, 'I never knew you; go away from me, you evildoers.'

■ ■ ■

It's God's world. He makes the rules. We chafe and squirm like restless adolescences, but that is the way it is. What God asks of us in our relationship with him is more than lip-service. What God asks of us is a life in which we speak what we believe and live what we speak with acts of love, justice, and mercy. A child knows what her parent values - what gives them joy and what makes them sad. As children of God we know that it gives God joy when we love well and intentionally. We also know it makes God sad when we just mouth the words. The worst words we could ever hear God utter to us are "Who are you?" Our baptismal promise is that God will always recognize us.

■ ■ ■

Holy God, you love us and call us by our name. Help us to respond to that gracious love with a life of integrity. Amen.

May 26

Hosea 6:1-3
Come, let us return to the Lord; for it is he who has torn,
and he will heal us; he has struck down, and he will bind us
up. After two days he will revive us; on the third day he will
raise us up, that we may live before him. Let us know, let
us press on to know the Lord; his appearing is as sure as
the dawn; he will come to us like the showers, like the
spring rains that water the earth.

■ ■ ■

The writings of the prophet Hosea portray the actions of the
people of Israel like a fickled lover who doesn't know what
is good for her, who seeks the company of those who would
use and harm her, and who continually forgets how faithful
God is. We can be easily distracted by the enticing ways of
the world or simply lazy in our relationship with God. It
would be callous of us to assume that God does not ache or
can easily dismiss our daily betrayals. It hurts. The grace of
it is that God continues to call us home, forgive us, revive
us, and promise us a life with him forever.

■ ■ ■

Prone to wander, Lord, we feel it....prone to leave you and
drift away to the matters that distract us. Help us to hear
your voice and return to you more quickly until that day
comes when we will never leave you again because of your
grace. Amen.

May 27

Acts 4:11-12
This Jesus is 'the stone that was rejected by you, the
builders; it has become the cornerstone.' There is a
salvation in no one else, for there is no other name under
heaven given among mortals by which we must be saved.

■ ■ ■

It is an ancient question that still vibrates in contemporary
conversations - Is there only one God? Is there only one true
faith? Is there only one way of salvation? Though we can
certainly engage in the debate in a philosophical manner,
we can only speak authoritatively on what we have seen
and heard. We have to operate on this side of the Kingdom
of Heaven according to the information we have. What we
have are the host of witnesses in the scriptures, throughout
history and amongst our own family, friends, and co-
workers. What we know is our own experience and
knowledge of grace undeserved and love beyond our
capacity to imagine. I would not dare to risk the peace
available to someone I love by saying, "Maybe there is
another god, another way." We are called to confess
according to what we have seen and heard. Jesus is Lord.

■ ■ ■

Holy God, we love to have options but help us to see that
what you offer to us in a relationship with you puts to rest
our restlessness. Amen.

May 28

Psalm 23
The Lord is my shepherd...

■ ■ ■

Without printing them here, the words and phrases of this psalm come floating to the surface of our consciousness like a familiar melody. We may not get the words in the right order or we might drop a phrase or two, but we know how this psalm makes us feel. From the first phrase we make a declaration in one breath that we need a shepherd and that we have one and that the one we have is God. From there we know rest, stillness, protection from evil, comfort, goodness and mercy, and a place to call home.

■ ■ ■

Follow us, Lord, all the days of our life and let us dwell in your house forever. Amen.

May 29

I John 3:23-24
And this is his commandment, that we should believe in the
name of his Son Jesus Christ and love one another, just as
he has commanded us. All who obey his commandments
abide in him, and he abides in them. And by this we know
that he abides in us, by the Spirit that he has given us.

■ ■ ■

Believe in Christ and love each other. It sounds so simple.
And it is. We are the ones who tend to make it complicated.
We take this Jesus and splay him on the dissection table of
our theological and philosophical lab. We turn love into a
squishy feeling that is impossible to reproduce and is as
fleeting as water through our fingers. Believe in Christ and
love each other. It is simple. It is a simple thing for us to
rise everyday and embrace these commandments with
courage and passion - to have faith in Christ and make love
real. At the end of the day, it gives us a way of evaluating
the gift of our lives. Did we believe Christ today? Did we
love? Each day will end in confession, forgiveness and each
day will begin with a renewed call to believe and love. Such
is the simple grace of the God who believes in us and loves
us relentlessly.

■ ■ ■

Holy God, may we believe you at your Word and love one
another in obedience to your command. Amen.

May 30

John 10:14-16
I am the good shepherd. I know my own and my own know
me, just as the Father knows me and I know the Father.
And I lay down my life for the sheep. I have other sheep
that do not belong to this fold. I must bring them also, and
they will listen to my voice.

■　■　■

We build our houses now with porches facing the backyards
and not toward the street or neighborhoods. We spend huge
amounts of time inside our cars. We rarely use dining
rooms but eat at different times and on the run. We feel the
disconnectedness of our lives from the people around us and
we long to be better neighbors and friends, but often don't
know how or when we can afford the time. Christ the
Shepherd gives us all his time. He is constantly accessible.
He is vigilant. He spends his time knowing us. When we
hear his voice, it is worth the time to listen. When we hear
his voice, we grow in our connection to all those who hear
him too.

■　■　■

Good shepherd, watch over us, know us and lead us in your
will. Amen.

May 31

John 12:35
Walk while you have the light, so that the darkness may
not overtake you.

■ ■ ■

Anyone who has ever been in an airplane at night knows about darkness and light. The lights of the city from above point out how massive our efforts are at punching holes in the darkness. It also reveals how feeble those efforts are. The night is a black fog that stifles the breath of tiny street lights. Even still, we flail at the darkness knowing that there is safety in what we can see. We are celestial warriors with light sabers standing defiantly against the fear of whatever would find darkness comforting. As we trip along through the shadowy paths of our lives, Jesus offers a light for our feet and freedom from our fear. He does not tell us that there is nothing to fear, for indeed, that which is evil is at home in the night. Jesus himself would be swallowed in the shadowy realm of death until the brilliant light of Easter. We live in a world still of darkness and light, of voices that call us to make choices that affect our lives and those around us. Jesus offers himself as the light of the world, so that we can choose well and know victory in the battle with the night.

■ ■ ■

Lord of Light, Shine on us that we may see the truth about who we are and who you are. Amen.

152

June 1

Acts 8:34-5
The eunuch asked Philip, "About whom, may I ask you,
does the prophet say this, about himself or about someone
else?" Then Philip began to speak, and starting with this
scripture, he proclaimed to him the good news about Jesus.

■ ■ ■

As a teacher of the Bible, I cringe when someone asks me a
question to which I must respond, "I don't know." My
limited educational credentials don't help me when we are
discussing a book that involves the disciplines of language,
geography, history, literary criticism, civilization,
agriculture, philosophy and theology. I know where to go to
look up the answer, but there is often just too much to know
to carry around it all around in my head. After centuries of
studying the Hebrew scriptures and not know what was
meant by a Messiah, those first century Christians were
finally given the opportunity to blow the dust off the
ancient words. There is and will always be much we don't
know but we will always be able to say, "I've heard of this
Jesus – let me tell you what I know."

■ ■ ■

Holy God, there is so much we don't know and too much
that we know that doesn't seem to matter. May the
knowledge of your Son alive in our lives inform us with the
Good News. Amen.

June 2

Psalm 22:26
The poor shall eat and be satisfied; those who seek him
shall praise the Lord.

■ ■ ■

I had a conversation once with a brilliant economist. I asked him, from his perspective as an economist, how the problem of poverty might be confronted. He told me one of the basic principles of economics is that everyone operates out of their own self-interest. Poverty could be addressed if enough resources were released by enough people whose self-interest was helping the poor. The economist didn't have any answers for how to make that happen. It is in turning to the Lord that we remember the depths of our blessings and can freely give out of those depths for the sake of others.

■ ■ ■

Lord, your kingdom come...your will be done on earth as it is in heaven. Amen.

June 3

I John 4:11-12
Beloved, since God loved us so much, we also ought to love
one another. No one has ever seen God; if we love one
another, God lives in us, and his love is perfected in us.

■ ■ ■

One Bible study curriculum I use states that as we study
the scriptures, we should always be asking, "Given what
God has done, what is he calling us to do and be." I have the
privilege of knowing some really remarkable mothers -
what makes them remarkable is that the love for their own
children is a part of the fiber of their being that it spills
over beyond their own households. They don't have to -
they just do. Given what God has done for us, he is calling
us to give love selflessly to the God-given relationships of
our families and to let it spill over onto our friends and
strangers even our enemies. There will be days when all
that love will feel in short supply, but the source of that
love never ceases to spill onto us. The scriptures, when we
are listening, call us to do more and be more than we could
ever imagine. The miracle of God's economy is that the
more we give, the more we have to give.

■ ■ ■

Who do you want us to love today, Lord? Show us how.
Amen.

155

June 4

John 15:4-5
Abide in me as I abide in you. Just as the branch cannot bear fruit by itself unless it abides in the vine, neither can you unless you abide in me. I am the vine, you are the branches. Those who abide in me and I in them bear much fruit, because apart from me you can do nothing.

■ ■ ■

Abide - the word by itself has a feeling of time, of lingering, of rest. Abiding doesn't happen in a hurry. We don't do "abiding" well in our busy culture. We do not linger long in any one spot. We do not stay well connected long enough to have the best of who we are become a part of another. Jesus gave us the picture of a vine and branches. Branches disconnected from the vine are only good as firewood. Connected to the vine, they are a part of the interaction of the energies of life forces passing through and creating new things. Abiding in Jesus is not just a luxury for those with discretionary time. It is a necessity of life.

■ ■ ■

Lord, if you are willing to rest and live inside the likes of us, help us to linger in you. Amen.

June 5

Matthew 20:15-16
Am I not allowed to do what I choose with what belongs to
me? Or are you envious because I am generous?" So the last
will be first, and the first will be last."

■　■　■

How did God know that over the years in our relationship
with him that we would arch our backs and throw toddler-
like tantrums over the issue of fairness? We want to know
that justice will be served, that the bad people will be
punished, that the good people will be rewarded, and no one
will be treated in a manner in which they do not deserve. I
dare say, if we were writing a blueprint for the plan of
salvation we wouldn't include things like the cross. After
all, Jesus was not treated justly. It wasn't fair that he died
a miserable death in order to save the world. Couldn't God
have fashioned a plan that was fairer, less messy? Jesus
tells a story that reveals that God's Kingdom is one in
which grace - not fairness - rules. God created the grace and
the ones who receive it. We can flail our arms in protest but
even if we could dream of a plan that was fairer we couldn't
pull it off. We are saved by grace by the power of God. It's
not fair but it is and will always be the best deal in town.

■　■　■

God of Grace, forgive our cries for fairness and transform
our hearts for compassion. Amen.

157

June 6

Acts 10:47-48
"Can anyone withhold the water for baptizing these people
who have received the Holy Spirit just as we have?" So he
ordered them to be baptized in the name of Jesus Christ.
Then they invited him to stay for several days.

■ ■ ■

Peter preached Christ to the Jews and to the non-Jews.
When the non-Jews responded in faith the Jews were taken
aback. How can this be that people "outside the family"
could understand family matters? To this day, the
connection of blood is as strong as ever. It is a part of the
fabric of our lives. It is one that God honors, blesses, and
creates. It is also God the Creator's prerogative to add new
threads and create new patterns in that holy fabric. God's
family is one defined less by blood and more by water and
the Spirit.

■ ■ ■

Bless our families, Lord, with your love and care and grant
us the wisdom to define family according to your will and
your ways. Amen.

June 7

John 10:37
If I am not doing the works of my Father, then do not believe me.

■ ■ ■

There are many good reasons why a person does a good work. It may be because the person likes how it makes her feel when she has done a good deed. Another reason may be that the kind act is good for the family or the community. A good work may be done because a person wants others to know that their community or their group is one which cares for others. No matter what the motivation, a good work is accomplished. The reason that Jesus did good works was yet another motivator - to glorify God. A kindness done in God's name has a power like the world has never known.

■ ■ ■

Lord, move us to great acts of kindness for the best of reasons. Amen.

June 8

Psalm 98:1
O sing to the Lord a new song, for he has done marvelous things.

■ ■ ■

From time to time, I ask people to tell me their recent "Wow" moments. Those are moments when we praise God simply because that is absolutely the finest response to something God made happen. It could be an awesome sunset, a beautiful child, a rose in bloom, or the feel of crisp morning air permeating our lungs. It could be the miracle of forgiveness or a flash of insight. To praise God is to have a mini-party in his honor at the spur of the moment. The shorter the time between those little celebrations, the more our lives take on the character of the Kingdom of Heaven.

■ ■ ■

Praise God from whom all blessing flow, Praise God all creatures here below. Amen.

June 9

Zephaniah 3:18b-20
I will remove disaster from you, so that you will not bear
reproach for it. I will deal with all your oppressors at that
time. And I will save the lame and gather the outcast, and I
will change their shame into praise and renown in all the
earth. At that time I will bring you home, at the time when
I gather you; for I will make you renowned and praised
among all the peoples of the earth, when I restore your
fortunes before your eyes, says the Lord.

■ ■ ■

Maya Angelou wrote a book that bore the name of one of
her poems, "I Know Why the Caged Bird Sings." Those who
are oppressed know how to sing the blues and also know
how to sing songs of hope in the face of the deepest despair.
The prophet's words are wonderful news for those who have
been undercut and misunderstood and laid low. There is
also a word that is not so good for the oppressors. The
challenge for us all is knowing that at any given time we
may be the lame and the outcast or we may be the one
kicking someone in the shins and causing the pain. God
comes for both the oppressed and the oppressors, but that is
only good news for one of them. I think I would rather be on
God's way than in it.

■ ■ ■

Holy God, convict us of our sin and redeem us with your
love. Amen.

June 10

John 12:47
For I came not to judge the world, but to save the world.

■ ■ ■

There are itinerant preachers who often come to university campuses to claim the public space for a couple hours. As thousands of students walk by, these people shout words of judgment. They slam the way the women are dressed or the way the men behave. Many of the students ignore the preachers. Some engage them in a loud and animated debate more for sport than a true exchange of understanding and ideas. But there is another group of victims of this abusive preaching that grieves my heart. I grieve the students who walk by the verbal assault already feeling worthless or guilty. Instead of hope, they hear cruel judgment spoken in Jesus' name. Jesus knew that judging would come rather naturally to us. We do it often and well. It's the loving part we have to practice more. We are called to show compassion not to broadcast our judgment.

■ ■ ■

Lord, make us slow to judge and quick to love. Amen.

June 11

Acts 1:21-24
So one of the men who have accompanied us during all the time that the Lord Jesus went in and out among us, beginning from the baptism of John until the day when he was taken up from us-one of these must become a witness with us to his resurrection." So they proposed two, Joseph called Barsabbas, who was also known as Justus, and Matthias. Then they prayed and said, "Lord, you know everyone's heart. Show us which one of these two you have chosen.

■ ■ ■

To fill the vacancy in their ranks, the apostles asked God for guidance and then they cast lots. They trusted that God would and could work his will through the flip of a coin. Such faith! Perhaps they knew these two so well that it really didn't matter which one was chosen. They were trying to honor a holy number of twelve. They were not creating a secret society or an exclusive club. They picked Matthias. Justus is believed to have remained and served Paul in his ministry. God's purposes were accomplished. We trust the Lord to know our heart but we don't often trust ourselves to truly see one another's. When the fog clears and the coin flips, God will make it right.

■ ■ ■

Holy God, may we trust in your will and your ways. Amen.

June 12

Psalm 1:1-3
Happy are those who do not follow the advice of the wicked, or take the path that sinners tread, or sit in the seat of scoffers; but their delight is in the law of the Lord, and on his law they meditate day and night. They are like trees planted by streams of water, which yield their fruit in its season, and their leaves do not wither.

■ ■ ■

We all know them. You know, those folks who never seem to have a good word to say about anything or anyone. They generate criticism with the ferocity of a wood chipper. We, of course, are never among them which is the insidious nature of negativism. We are up to our armpits in it ourselves before we notice, if ever, that we are aiding and abetting this joy thief. We would be wise to be attentive to how we move through our day, with whom we spend our time, and where we draw our source of truth and hope. It all determines what kind of aroma we leave behind us. By the river of God's truth, we can plant ourselves and provide the fragrance of his joy and love.

■ ■ ■

Holy God, fill us with all things good, so that we might be the bearers of delight in a weary world. Amen.

June 13

John 17:15-16
I am not asking you to take them out of the world, but I ask
you to protect them from the evil one. They do not belong to
the world, just as I do not belong to the world. Sanctify
them in the truth; your word is truth.

■ ■ ■

God created the world and called it good. It still is good. Everywhere one looks it is charged with the grandeur of God. The world is not evil, but evil exists. It is easy to see the grandeur of God in a morning glory tilting its face to the sun or in an oak tree etched into a pink and azure early evening sky. Evil is around and within us snapping us to attention with a whisper. The challenge for the faithful is to reside in one place, but to cling to the identity of our citizenship in another realm even when the lines are sometimes blurred.

■ ■ ■

Help us to know and claim who we are in your, Lord. Amen.

June 14

Mark 9:42
If any of you put a stumbling block before one of these little ones who believe in me, it would be better for you if a great millstone were hung around your neck and you were thrown into the sea.

■ ■ ■

When we were children, we would play in the living room oblivious to the fact that we were in front of the television that my father was trying to watch. We would hear him say in a calm voice without a hint of anger, "You make a better door than you do a window." It always took us a few seconds to understand that he could not see through us and we should get out of the way. We can't be God for anyone, but we can clear the way for someone to see the Christ who loves, forgives, and redeems. Not often enough do we consider our words and actions which might pose obstacles for someone's faith. Our most sincere efforts to help can be muddied by our need to control. We make a significant step of growth when we recognize that we may be a part of the problem and not the solution. Grace and forgiveness are the hinges on which we can swing to stay connected and humbly getting out of the way.

■ ■ ■

Lord, grant me the wisdom to know when to help and when to get out of the way. Amen.

June 15

John 11:47-48
So the chief priests and the Pharisees called a meeting of the council, and said, "What are we to do? This man is performing many signs. If we let him go on like this, everyone will believe in him, and the Romans will come and destroy both our holy place and our nation."

■ ■ ■

Don't rock the boat. Keep the status quo. The Jews knew that Jesus was a powerful force for change in their midst. Even though they were oppressed by the Romans, they had learned to live inside the tension of their lack of freedom. If they were quiet, the Romans left them alone. Jesus threatened to rock their world. They didn't want to change. They had learned to live within the fear and the Roman restraint however unfair. Jesus would focus the attention of Rome on them. They chose to view Jesus as the enemy and began to orchestrate the political moves to bring about his death. We have to deal with change every day. Even to keep the status quo and to maintain our lives requires constant changes and maneuvering. Like a swimmer who treads water, it takes a good deal of energy to stay in the same place. Jesus offers a life with changes to be made, energy spent, and the boat rocked. We can live with a rocking boat. It all has to do with who is rocking it.

■ ■ ■

Lord God, rock our world with your grace. Amen.

June 16

Isaiah 12:2-4
Surely God is my salvation; I will trust, and will not be
afraid, for the Lord God is my strength and my might, and
has become my salvation. With joy you will draw water
from the wells of salvation. And you will say in that day:
Give thanks to the Lord, call on God's name; make known
the deeds of the Lord among the nations; proclaim that this
name is exalted.

■ ■ ■

"Surely God is my salvation, I will trust..." It sounds like someone about to walk into a courtroom or a job interview or a first date or a final exam. Think positive! So says our refrigerator magnets or bumper stickers or perpetually optimistic friends. Psychologists tell us that over 70% of our "internal speak" is negative. We need those voices that have a positive, hopeful message to hammer at our negativity and get us to lighten up. I have the blessing of friends with the gift of exhortation - the gift of encouraging others with the hope born in the Spirit of our Lord. After a while, the voice of hope begins to sound like our own.

■ ■ ■

Holy God, speak to us that we may speak in living echoes of your hope. Amen.

June 17

Psalm 50:14
Offer to God a sacrifice of thanksgiving and make good your vows to the Most High. Call upon me in the day of trouble; I will deliver you, and you shall honor me.

■ ■ ■

I picked up a prescription I needed and the pharmacist highlighted the important things to remember when taking the medicine. The instructions told me when to take it, how often, and what foods to avoid while I take it and what side-effects it might cause. The bottom line is still that the drug, when taken correctly, is good for me. There are a few occasions in which God is prescriptive with us. There are places and times in the scriptures when he says "Do this." Communion is one. Baptism is another. And we are told to love God will all our heart, mind, and strength and our neighbor as ourselves. God writes us a prescription that says "Say Thanks - several times a day." The side-effects are all splendid.

■ ■ ■

Lord God, thank you, thank you, thank you! Amen.

June 18

Matthew 9: 10-13
And as he sat at dinner in the house, many tax collectors
and sinners came and were sitting with him and his
disciples. When the Pharisees saw this, they said to his
disciples, "Why does your teacher eat with tax collectors
and sinners?" But when he heard this, he said, "Those who
are well have no need of a physician, but those who are
sick. Go and learn what this means, 'I desire mercy, not
sacrifice.' For I have come to call not the righteous but
sinners."

■ ■ ■

For much of my life, I have been a master at the sarcastic
remark. I hear questions like the one the Pharisees asked
and my head comes up with a bunch of smart, witty, often
snotty retorts that only tease or slam and never answer the
question. Jesus' response to the Pharisees is pointed, not
the kind of answer they were expecting and it wasn't
sarcasm but mercy. Sometimes the difference between the
merciful response and the hard-hearted one is simply
taking a moment to realize that we are the guest of honor
at a dinner for sinners.

■ ■ ■

Massage our hearts, Lord, so that they may not turn to
stone but pulse with mercy for a world that needs your love
and forgiveness. Amen.

170

June 19

Exodus 19:7-8
But you shall be for me a priestly kingdom and a holy
nation. So Moses came, summoned the elders of the people,
and set before them all these words that the Lord had
commanded him. The people all answered as one:
"Everything that the Lord has spoken we will do."

■ ■ ■

I am tempted to add a sarcastic "Yeah, right" to the people's
response to God's command. The people responded with one
voice with good intentions, but one at a time they peeled off
at the edges. We do that when we think our singular
presence makes no difference to whole. We think it doesn't
matter whether we contribute nor do we think we can do
the whole community any harm with our singular bad
behavior. We may even imagine ourselves to be invisible.
Just as God notices a sparrow when it falls to the ground or
can count hairs, God notices when we disconnect ourselves
from his people and his mission. No matter what we think,
we matter.

■ ■ ■

Holy God, your ability to attend to the details of your
creation amazes us. Help us to be attentive to the details of
love and mercy. Amen.

171

June 20

Psalm 100:1-2
Be joyful in the Lord, all you lands; serve the Lord with
gladness and come before his presence with a song.

■ ■ ■

This is unabashedly one of my favorite psalms. Whenever I
read it, I hear what I need to hear about being joyful,
serving with gladness, and reveling in God's presence in our
lives. It tells us who we are and who God is and how to
move around in that relationship. More often than not, we
speak of our relationship with God as if we are running
away, hiding, ashamed, angry, or confused. Relationships
are like that, but in the good ones we want to be in one
another's presence. There is joy in simply that. The rough
patches we will work out together. We have lots of time.

■ ■ ■

Lord God, thank you for flinging open the doors and
windows of your heart to welcome us in our shabby state
every single day of your life. Amen.

June 21

Romans 5:3-5
And not only that, but we also boast in our sufferings,
knowing that suffering produces endurance, and endurance
produces character, and character produces hope, and hope
does not disappoint us, because God's love has been poured
into our hearts through the Holy Spirit that has been given
to us.

■ ■ ■

Sometimes the Apostle Paul's ability to spin-doctor a bad situation into a good one drives me crazy. He would regularly write that his sufferings were a joy because they helped him to be more intimately connected to Christ's cross. I am not so noble when it comes to suffering - my own or others. I just want the suffering to stop. I am less concerned in the moment about endurance, character, and hope. I want the quick fix. The happy pill. I want to fast-forward to the warm, fuzzy part. But as much as I hate to admit it...Paul was right. To see our sufferings as a way in which we share the cross of Christ is to know love at its best and strongest and most victorious. Love will always trump sin and suffering.

■ ■ ■

Lord God, we often like to tell you what to do and how to do it. Forgive us. Help us to embrace our lives, confess our sin, endure our suffering, and believe your love. Amen.

173

June 22

Matthew 9: 37-38
Then he said to his disciples, "The harvest is plentiful, but
the laborers are few; therefore ask the Lord of the harvest
to send out laborers into his harvest.

■ ■ ■

I chatted with a person in the parking lot of the post office
one morning. Her son was thinking about the ministry as a
vocation. The job of a pastor can be complicated, requiring a
variety of skills and gifts that no one possesses completely.
It is a role embattled by credibility issues in our present
culture and filled with high expectations. Of the pastors I
have known, the ones who love God and love God's people
consistently honor God's call to a life of service. Our world
is filled with hurting, needy people and pastors can't
respond to all of the needs adequately. It needs everyone to
respond to the call to ministry at our baptism to love God
and love God's people every day.

■ ■ ■

Lord God, may everything we do today and every
conversation reflect our love for you and our love for your
people. Amen.

June 23

Jeremiah 20:9
If I say, "I will not mention him, or speak any more in his name," then within me there is something like a burning fire shut up in my bones; I am weary with holding it in, and I cannot.

■ ■ ■

Jeremiah was a prophet whose job it was to deliver constant warnings to a people who couldn't care less. He was the laughingstock of the community. He was chided by his friends. He was lonely and miserable most of the time. He regularly complained to God. He saw little results for his daily labors. There were days when he wanted to pull the blanket over his head and forget everything. There were days when he wanted to quit being God's prophet. And yet, he describes how he can't help but speak. The Spirit of the living God was at work in the melancholy prophet and in everyone who has made known that Spirit to us. The question then becomes for us today....are we in God's way or on it?

■ ■ ■

Holy God, stir us up this day that we cannot but speak of the truth and grace we have known in you. Amen.

June 24

Psalm 69:14-15
Save me from the mire; do not let me sink; let me be
rescued from those who hate me and out of the deep waters.
Let not the torrent of waters wash over me, neither let the
deep swallow me up; do not let the pit shut its mouth upon
me.

■ ■ ■

Occasionally I let my pet parrot out of his cage. He normally just sits on top of it and takes in the scenery but if frightened he flies to the other side of the room and drops to the floor. Uncertain of his surroundings, he looks at me and lifts up his claw and says "Up!" - meaning "Please pick me up and put me back where I belong!" The psalmist vividly captures the feeling of a person overwhelmed with problems. Who among us has not known that icky drowning feeling when we seem over our heads with everything from serious, life-threatening issues to piles of daily details? God allows us to look to him and say "Up!" Remarkably those who cry "Up!" will have their prayers answered with the strength and patience to endure more than we could ever imagine.

■ ■ ■

Holy God, we cry to you and lift our arms to you from the pit. Thank you for hearing our prayer and raising us up. Amen.

June 25

Romans 6:10-11
The death he died, he died to sin, once for all; but the life he lives, he lives to God. So you also must consider yourselves dead to sin and alive to God in Christ Jesus.

■ ■ ■

Death still wreaks havoc. The daily headlines remind us of death's rampage through suicide bombers, budgets that never adequately address human suffering, natural disaster death tolls, or the sick behavior of everyone from politicians to rock stars. Obituaries happen every day. The other news we are called to report to the world is one that declares that death no longer has dominion. Even as we sin and carry the curse of death within us, we are also alive in Christ. We can walk around in our death or we can consider ourselves alive. Christ is alive! What fun to be the bearers of such good news!

■ ■ ■

Living God, we rejoice today that you are victorious over sin and death and have offered to us the cross of Christ so that we might live to tell the story. Amen.

June 26

Matthew 10:29,31
Are not two sparrows sold for a penny? Yet not one of them
will fall to the ground apart from your Father. So do not be
afraid; you are of more value than many sparrows.

■ ■ ■

"Mr. Cellophane" in the musical "Chicago" sings "you can
look right through me, walk right by me and never know
I'm there." We have all had our cellophane days. When they
string together they become a slippery slope of despair or a
lousy attitude. The vivid message of Christ to his disciples
is that each of them have significance and value. If God is
attentive to a tiny bird, then so much more so, God notices
us. There is very little wiggle room in that logic. God makes
it clear.

■ ■ ■

Holy God, thank you for listening to the sound of a sparrow
and attending to its needs so that we might know that your
heart is big enough to love us even when we feel small.
Amen.

178

June 27

Jeremiah 28:6-7
And the prophet Jeremiah said, "Amen.! May the Lord do so; may the Lord fulfill the words that you have prophesied, and bring back to this place from Babylon the vessels of the house of the Lord, and all the exiles. But listen now to this word that I speak in your hearing and in the hearing of all the people."

■ ■ ■

In the television series "Star Trek: The Next Generation" Captain Jean-Luc Picard would often issue an order to his first officer by saying, "Make it so, Number One!" The word 'Amen.' in Hebrew could be loosely translated "make it so." We punctuate our prayers with this simple word of affirmation, hope, and even a little urgency. Jeremiah would later speak of a prophet of peace unlike any other that Israel has known. The "number one" prophet who could do more than just speak of the need for change and offer warnings. This prophet could make God's will so. When we are in need of love and grace and forgiveness, we can look to the cross of Christ and offer our prayer "Make it so, Number One."

■ ■ ■

Holy God, refresh this day with new reminders that we are called, chosen, loved and sent. Amen.

June 28

Psalm 89:1-2
Your love, O Lord, forever will I sing; from age to age my mouth will proclaim your faithfulness. For I am persuaded that your love is established forever; you have set your faithfulness firmly in the heavens.

■ ■ ■

Time, like real estate, is precious because we can't make more than what we have been given. Even still, we dream of a time when we will have all the time in the world and that we ourselves might be defined as being forever people. We boldly claim that we will love our loved ones forever as if we own forever. But time is not something that can be stockpiled or invested for a return at a later date. God gives us this amazing promise of life forever in him - it is not given to us to waste, to treat casually, or to abuse - it has been given to us to savor, to love one another well and to make justice happen right now. How long we get to do this is entirely up to the One who owns all of time.

■ ■ ■

Lord God, help us to measure our days with the quality of our relationships, the nobility of our service to others, and with the number of ways we thank you for our life. Amen.

June 29

Romans 6: 13-14
But present yourselves to God as those who have been brought from death to life, and present your members to God as instruments of righteousness. For sin will have no dominion over you, since you are not under the law but under grace.

■　■　■

One of the great weapons of the demonic is the ability to adjust the volume levels inside our heads. We are a fickled, sinful lot who will turn our heads to just about any voice. Not all of those voices are good nor do all have our best interest in mind. We are easily led to say or do the wrong thing. We are distracted from God's voice. To present ourselves to God means in part, that we are ready to listen - that we are willing to turn down the volume of other noise and let his voice of love shape our lives.

■　■　■

Lord God, we are tired of the sound of our own voice leading us in mental circles, thoughtless words and acts, and wasted hours. We present ourselves to you today - our whole selves. Amen.

June 30

Matthew 10:41-42
And whoever welcomes a righteous person in the name of a
righteous person will receive the reward of the righteous;
and whoever gives given a cup of cold water to one of these
little ones in the name of a disciple - truly I tell you, none of
these will lose their reward.

■ ■ ■

I was taking a flight to a city in another state for a meeting.
The flight was delayed. I not only missed the first session of
the meeting - everyone had left for the night and I was
unsure about my accommodations at a retreat center. With
the help of a kind taxi driver, I found the meeting room, a
note on the table, a key to a room. I would have preferred a
hug from a familiar friend, a cup of coffee, a hand with my
luggage, and a nice conversation, but the kindness, the note
and the key was just enough welcome to know that I was
expected, missed, and belonged. Jesus did not
underestimate the power of a simple gesture of making
space for a guest in our lives. Neither should we.

■ ■ ■

Holy God, as we were welcomed into your family with water
and your word, help us to welcome those who come and go
who need a place, if only for a moment, to belong. Amen.

July 1

Zechariah 9:11-12
As for you also, because of the blood of my covenant with you, I will set your prisoners free from the waterless pit. Return to your stronghold, O prisoners of hope; today I declare that I will restore to you double.

■ ■ ■

What's your stronghold? We all know the importance of one. We all need a stronghold when life feels more like a battle than a walk in the park. Strongholds are where we go to get a breather, reload, treat our wounds, assess our strategy, attend to the people fighting with us side by side. For some people, it is an actual place. For some it is the blessed presence of a person who makes no demands but offers themselves as shelter and a solid soul on whom we can lean. Inside that space we leave our empty shells, our dirty clothes, our bloody rags. Inside that stronghold we gird ourselves with the knowledge that the fight is worth it and that we are able. Thanks be to God who is our stronghold. The battle is worth it and we are able.

■ ■ ■

Lord God, thank you for your Son, our stronghold in the fight. Help us to be strong enough to hold someone who needs the grace of our space. Amen.

July 2

Psalm 145:8-9
The Lord is gracious and full of compassion, slow to anger
and of great kindness. The Lord is loving to everyone and
his compassion is over all his works.

■ ■ ■

Philosophers when speaking of the idea of God have referred to him as "Prime Mover." All the forces that are at work in the world had to have a beginning. Something or someone gave the world, at least, a first push. Our Prime Mover continues to push us like an untiring parent standing in back of a child's swing. Such an act is unselfish, motivated by the joy of another, requiring an attentive eye and a gentle hand. We are children when it comes to love. We need to be taught how to do it well. Sometimes we need to remember why we do it at all. God, our prime mover, pushes us with love for the sake of love.

■ ■ ■

Holy God, thank you for being so gentle with us. Keep pushing us to reach beyond ourselves to carry into our days the power of your grace and compassion. Amen.

July 3

Romans 7:24-25
Wretched man that I am! Who will rescue me from this
body of death? Thanks be to God through Jesus Christ our
Lord!

■ ■ ■

The Apostle Paul in his letter to the Romans wrote the most
eloquent theological essays on the nature of sin and the
power of grace. The thunder of his witness resounds
through the testimony of his own life. Paul takes a tough
stand on the destructive character of sin, but he does it
while confessing his own enslavement to it. What we all
have in common is our sinfulness. What we all need is to be
rescued. Not even Paul - an apostle of Jesus Christ - a
martyr of the faith - a champion for the Gospel - can rescue
us since he needed rescuing himself. We have a savior.
Thanks be to God. The battle with our sinfulness still rages
but we have been put on the winning side.

■ ■ ■

Holy God, we are not worthy of anything but criticism and
punishment for all that we do, think, and leave undone.
Forgive us and embrace us to bring honor to your name.
Amen.

July 4

Matthew 11:28-30
Come to me, all you that are weary and are carrying heavy
burdens, and I will give you rest. Take my yoke upon you,
and learn from me; for I am gentle and humble in heart,
and you will find rest for your souls. For my yoke is easy,
and my burden is light.

■　■　■

It doesn't make much sense to trade one burden for
another. It doesn't make sense until we try it. My burden is
unwieldy, cumbersome, impossible for one person to hold all
at once. The yoke of Jesus' burden is no less heavy and it is
still impossible for us to carry alone, but the yoke of Jesus
comes with Jesus himself. And that makes all the
difference.

■　■　■

Lord, keep us from becoming so attached to our burdens
that we don't trust your cross or have room in our arms to
hold your weary ones. Amen.

July 5

Psalm 104:25-26
O Lord, how manifold are your works! In wisdom you have made them all; the earth is full of your creatures. Yonder is the great and wide sea with its living things too many to number, creatures both small and great. There move the ships, and there is that Leviathan, which you have made for the sport of it. All of them look to you and give them their food in due season.

■ ■ ■

I watched a television program the other day about creatures in the wilderness. The commentator introduced another animal by saying "And some creatures have the benefit of living in their very own salad bowl...." The image on the screen was that of what appeared to be a field of lush green plants. The gaping mouth of a hippopotamus suddenly appeared from below chomping up the watery greenery. I love watching those animal shows and walking through zoos. There is no more obvious example of God's immense imagination, except of course, if we consider the people with whom you live and work.

■ ■ ■

For all the creatures great and small and the variety of our world, we give you thanks and enjoy your imagination, O Lord our God. Amen.

July 6

Isaiah 6:5,8
And I said: "Woe is me! I am lost, for I am a man of unclean
lips, and I live among a people of unclean lips; yet my eyes
have seen the King, the Lord of hosts!" Then I heard the
voice of the Lord saying, "Whom shall I send, and who will
go for us?" And I said, "Here am I; send me!"

■ ■ ■

Most of the time we have the luxury of periods of denial
especially when it comes to acknowledging our own sin.
When standing in the presence of the Lord any attempt at
denial will look really foolish. Isaiah is quick to admit his
sin and his utter amazement that he is still alive in the
presence of the one who could crush him like a gnat. The
prophet's sins are forgiven and God seems to muse out loud
wondering who he can send to deliver the message to his
people. The one who understands the depth of grace in his
life is quick to say, "Send me!" To understand grace is to
know that the next breath we take - and the one after that
and the one after that -is a gift. When the one who gave us
that breath calls us out to help in his mission, what better
use of that breath than to use it to say, "Yes!"

■ ■ ■

Giver of all Life, forgive our sins and send us to those who
need your saving grace. Amen.

July 7

Psalm 29:8,10-11

The voice of the Lord makes the oak trees writhe and strips the forests bare. The Lord shall strength to his people; the Lord shall give strength to his people; The Lord shall give his people the blessing of peace.

■ ■ ■

I recall a moment speaking to a teenager and an unchecked word of criticism flew from my mouth. It had the effect of stripping bark off a tree. Her countenance wilted before my eyes. I witnessed in a heartbeat the power of a word to wound the soul. I regretted it immediately and began the slow labor of restoring the relationship. Strength is something we pray for often but the form the strength takes in us is important. God can handle the business of judgment because he can do it without causing us to bleed out. God offers us the kind of strength that brings peace. Would that the words that fly from our mouths did not ride on razors.

■ ■ ■

Make us instruments, Lord, of your peace. Amen.

July 8

Romans 8:15
For you did not receive a spirit of slavery to fall back into
fear, but you have received a spirit of adoption. When we
cry, "Abba, Father!"

■ ■ ■

From childhood, our drive to belong is incredibly strong. We
recognize the voice and the face of the humans that belong
to us. We are keenly aware, in our teenage years into our
adulthood, of where we do and don't belong.. At any given
time, that awareness either creates anxiety or puts us at
peace. In a culture were boundaries surround families,
individuals, and groups, the anxiety of belonging or not
belonging is a daily event. The Lord hears our lonely cry
and lets us know that we belong to him.

■ ■ ■

Abba, Father, thank you for adopting us as your children.
Amen.

July 9

John 3:16-17
For God so loved the world that he gave his only Son, so that everyone who believes in him may not perish but may have eternal life. Indeed, God did not send the Son into the world to condemn the world, but in order that the world might be saved through him.

■　■　■

That we are condemned and that we need to be saved is a fact that often daily slaps us in the head. It may come in the irritating doubt of our own worth or the graceless voice of another person. We spend our days moving our guilt around like unwanted vegetables on a child's plate. The God who makes it possible for us to see our sin also forgives and sets us free. Sometimes we get so consumed with the bad news that we stop reading. With God, we need to keep reading and we need to keep hearing the Good News.

■　■　■

Thank you, Lord, for not giving up on us. Amen.

July 10

John 12:21
Sir, we wish to see Jesus.

■　■　■

It started with a sign of turning water into wine at a party. Then it was a healing here and driving demons out there. Soon the crowd began to build. Now Greeks, not Jews, were trying to make an appointment to see him. Jesus looked at his appointments and knew there was one in Jerusalem that he had to keep no matter who it was that needed to see him. The mission of Jesus was to save the world. He healed the sick, had power over demons, and made water into wine to make disciples in the short run. In the long run, those deeds were a sign, like the trailers for coming attractions at the movie theatre. When the Greeks arrived on the scene, it meant that Jesus was touching the lives of those far beyond Israel. Jesus' mission was not to meet with a few Greeks but to bring God's saving word to the world and to all generations. The time for the cross was at hand. The Greeks wanted to see Jesus, but in Christ's book, he had another appointment with the likes of you and me.

■　■　■

Lord God, when you sent Christ to the cross you had us in your mind and heart. Thank you! Amen.

July 11

Ezekiel 17:22-23
Thus says the Lord God: I myself will take a sprig from the
lofty top of a cedar; I will set it out. I will break off the
tender one from the topmost of its young twigs; I myself will
plant it on a high and lofty mountain. On the mountain
height of Israel I will plant it, in order that it may produce
boughs and bear fruit, and become a noble cedar.

■　■　■

With some help, I planted new trees in my backyard.. At
first, the trees lost leaves after the shock of the move and
slowly started to recover. I didn't think the re-planting
would be such a stressful event for them but apparently it
was. My skills as a pastor were totally useless. I could not
comfort them or tell them everything was going to be all
right. The business of planting and growing a people of God
is often one in which we can do certain things and fret over
it, but God makes the growth happen in his own time and
for his own purposes. Sometimes the best thing a tree
owner or a Christian can do is wait and trust.

■　■　■

Holy God, plant us where you need us and give us the
growth we need to be your fruitful people. Amen.

July 12

Psalm 92:1-2
It is a good thing to give thanks to the Lord, and to sing
praises to your name, O Most High; to tell of your loving
kindness early in the morning and of your faithfulness in
the night season on the psaltery, and on the lyre, and to the
melody of the harp.

■ ■ ■

I watched the Academy awards one year and before they
gave the award for musical score, they demonstrated the
importance of the musical score in a movie by showing a
clip with only the action and dialogue. It looked and
sounded a little too much like ...life. It was not enjoyable. I
have often wondered what our lives might be like if they
were scored with music. A light flute in the morning as we
picked up the paper from the driveway or trumpet after
receiving great news or a woeful violin blanketing our sad
shoulder. On the days when I get most stuck in knowing
how to pray, I sing. To add a score to our own lives is to
pray and praise and enter God's presence. God gives us an
endless supply of reasons to give thanks and to sing.

■ ■ ■

Follow us through our day, O Lord, and surround us with
the music of your grace. Amen.

July 13

Psalm 112:7
They are not afraid of evil tidings; their hearts are firm,
secure in the LORD.

■　■　■

On a youth group rafting trip, we were in several rafts with experienced guides. As we went through areas of rapids and stretches of calm water, the guides would lift their paddles high in the air. Later, I learned that it was the guides' way of communicating with each other that everything was okay. The tool they needed to survive was also the tool that spread hope. The trip would have been at best uncomfortable, at worst perilous had not the guide been with us. They still needed to have our oars in the water and obeying the rules for the sake of everyone in the raft. The purpose of the trip was adventure and we could not set out on it if we did not respect the river, trust the guide and appreciate our participation in the journey. God is, indeed, our ever-present guide, who asks us to respect the rules of the dominion and who invites us into the adventure. The cross of Jesus Christ is God's "Oars Up" to a frightened world to let us know that all is well, there is hope.

■　■　■

God, may we embrace our journey with you with shouts of joy. Amen.

July 14

Mark 4:30-32
He also said, "With what can we compare the kingdom of
God, or what parable will we use for it? It is like a mustard
seed, which, when sown upon the ground, is the smallest of
all the seeds on earth; yet when it is sown it grows up and
becomes the greatest of all shrubs, and puts forth large
branches, so that the birds of the air can make nests in the
shade."

■ ■ ■

Jesus told many parables to give us a glimpse of the
kingdom of God. No one story captured it all. Each story
had important elements we could use to imagine it. If we
try to imagine the kingdom's size, it will confound us. It
could be small, it could be growing, it could be huge. We are
not to underestimate the power of God to work even in the
smallest of circumstances or in people or even in a word or
a simple action. From such tiny bits of grace, the Kingdom
grows for us all.

■ ■ ■

Holy God, use the smallness of who we are to grow spaces
for everyone in your kingdom. Amen.

July 15

John 3: 35
The Father loves the Son and has placed all things in his hands.

■ ■ ■

As a campus pastor, I once had the responsibility of advising a group of students whose task it was to choose scholarship recipients. They did not know any of the students personally and had only the application and an essay to make their decision. There was no obvious winner and I watched the students agonize with their deliberations. The discussion was complicated by their inability to come to consensus about what they valued the most. They were also learning what it was like to be on the other end of a process in which they were usually the applicants. They walked away from the experience with a new respect for those put in the position to make choices. There is no greater burden God laid on his Son than the judgment of the world. Jesus agonized over it and in the end took on the punishment himself. Jesus was given the responsibility to choose and Jesus chose us.

■ ■ ■

God of Mercy, remind us of the mercy of the cross when we are called to stand in judgment. Amen.

July 16

Job 38:2-4
Who is this that darkens counsel by words without knowledge? Gird up your loins like a man, I will question you, and you shall declare to me. Where were you when I laid the foundation of the earth? Tell me, if you have understanding.

■ ■ ■

One of the interesting chapters of Bill Bryson's "A Short History of Nearly Everything" is the account of the scientific endeavor to determine the weight of the earth. Decades of research, entire careers were spent to find a single number. Some would argue that the target sum was less the topic of the research as the process to calculate it. Nevertheless, it is an example of the fact that we have the gifts and skills to have a certain level of dominion. However, it is still miniscule in the light of the one who created that dominion. There is a fine line between arrogance, humiliation, and true humility. We can only linger in true humility when we are aware of the presence and the nature of God.

■ ■ ■

Grant us the will and the wisdom to stand in your presence and not forget to kneel. Amen.

July 17

Psalm 107:25,27-30
Then he spoke, and a stormy wind arose, which tossed high
the waves of the sea. They reeled and staggered like
drunkards and were at their wits' end. Then they cried to
the Lord in their trouble, and he delivered them from their
distress. He stilled the storm to a whisper and quieted the
waves of the sea. Then were they glad because of the calm,
and he brought them to the harbor they were bound for.

■ ■ ■

We were a handful of passengers on a freighter approaching
Australia when the captain in a cautionary way asked if we
were ready for the "Tasman Dance." The Tasman Sea is a
particularly rough one to cross and the dance to which he
referred was how we would look walking about the ship
trying to keep our balance. We learned again about the
power of the sea to toss a multi-ton container ship like a
cork. When we turned into Melbourne Harbor everything
changed...the waters were glassy, calm, and silent as we
created a silky wake to our port. It is the memory of rough
seas and quiet harbors that build trust in God's comfort and
care.

■ ■ ■

Holy God, when we are in quiet harbors help us to
appreciate the peace you give us and when we are in rough
seas help us to remember your promises. Amen.

July 18

2 Corinthians 6:1,11
As we work together with him, we urge you also not to accept the grace of God in vain.....We have spoken frankly to you Corinthians; our heart is wide open to you. There is no restriction in our affection, but only in yours. In return - I speak as to children - open wide your hearts also.

■ ■ ■

I love the way Paul dove into his ministry among the cantankerous, twisted, and sometimes totally clueless Corinthians. He spent more time with them than any other place. He wrote more letters than we have in our possession to read. They were Paul's troubled children, requiring tough love, constant attention, and a firm hand. When we are wise, we listen to Paul as he admonishes the Christians of Corinth and admire him for being a model of vulnerability and service. When we are truly wise, we recognize that we are those stubborn Corinthians being reminded again of the depth, breadth, and magnitude of God's grace.

■ ■ ■

Lord, you who have never held back an ounce of love for us, teach us again in this day to love without restriction. Amen.

July 19

Mark 4:39
He woke up and rebuked the wind, and said to the sea,
"Peace! Be still!" Then the wind ceased, and there was a
dead calm.

■ ■ ■

I heard of an Oklahoma housewife who in her suicide note blamed the wind that blew relentlessly for her emotional spiral into the abyss of hopelessness. My mother experienced a hurricane as a child and carried her fear of the wind into her adulthood. Anyone who has ever flown knows what it is like to be buffeted about by a headwind or a crosswind or a down draft. The sea is just a giant puddle of water that sways with the tides, but with the force of the wind, it becomes a life-threatening monster. One of the Texas phrases I love is "If only the wind would just sit down." I don't know anyone who could not relate being hammered with the wind to something going on in their lives. We have all known and continue to know a relentless wind of troubles, burdens, events that sap our energy. We forget that just because Jesus is sleeping doesn't mean that he isn't dealing with the wind. His sleep tells us that we have nothing to fear. His rebuke of the wind tells us....he is bigger than the wind.

■ ■ ■

Lord, make the wind sit down in our lives so that we can rest and rejoice in the power of your name. Amen.

July 20

John 3:11
Very truly, I tell you, we speak of what we know and testify to what we have seen.

■ ■ ■

There was an article in a sports magazine about a famous football player who made a dramatic comeback after a long dark time of drug abuse and bad behavior. The player pointed to Christ as being the person who turned his life around. The sports writer had seen this story before and took a skeptical approach to his interview with the player and the investigation into his life past and present. At the end of the article, the writer admitted that even though one may doubt that Christ had anything to do with this football player, it is difficult to refute the testimony of a changed life. As of times of old, we still speak of what we have seen and heard. I have seen lives changed through hope, prayer, healing, and forgiveness. I have been changed by the daily reminders of God's grace.

■ ■ ■

Lord help us to remember that we can indeed change the world, one person at a time, starting and never ending with ourselves every day. Amen.

July 21

Lamentations 3:25-26
The Lord is good to those who wait for him, to the soul that seeks him. It is good that one should wait quietly for the salvation of the Lord.

■　■　■

Okay.....it sounded nice and do-able until I got to the "wait quietly" part. My head and my heart are a rambling cacophony of conversation with the Lord in which I do most of the talking and I repeat myself ....alot. I spend a considerable amount of energy saying, "Come, Lord Jesus!" and there is not much that is quiet about the request. I spend my days looking for him and grateful that I get glimpses in those who go the extra mile in surprising and wonderful ways for no other reason than the joy of knowing Jesus Christ. It is good to wait for the Lord. It is good for my soul to seek him. It is also good to wait quietly.....that way, just maybe, the Lord can get a word in edgewise.

■　■　■

Holy God, we trust and wait and seek your face. Thank you for listening to us and making yourself known. Amen.

July 22

Matthew 16: 19
I will give you the keys of the kingdom of heaven

■ ■ ■

The notion of St. Peter standing at the pearly gates granting or denying entrance comes from the imagery of Peter being given the "keys of the kingdom." Peter as heaven's gatekeeper is the opening line of hundreds of jokes. It is more likely that Jesus was referring to Peter's vital role in the proclamation of grace and forgiveness. Peter would have the opportunity to proclaim the Gospel of Jesus Christ to thousands of people. The result of that preaching is that thousands came to believe Christ. Peter established an important precedent of public witness. Christ also provided a key leader for the disciples before they began to scatter and begin their public ministries. We don't need to worry about an encounter with Peter at the gates of heaven. He may indeed be there but only because he is so good at pointing the way.

■ ■ ■

Thank you, Lord, for all the saints like Peter on whose shoulder we ride on our journey of faith. Amen.

July 23

2 Corinthians 8:13-15
I do not mean that there should be relief for others and
pressure on you, but it is a question of a fair balance
between your present abundance and their need, so that
their abundance may be for your need, in order that there
may be a fair balance. As it is written, "The one who had
much did not have too much, and the one who had little did
not have too little."

■ ■ ■

There was news one day of a multi-billionaire who gave
billions of dollars to a foundation established by another
multi-billionaire who gave much of his own billions to the
project. From the perspective of most of us, they live in a
land of a different digit in which the decimal point is a
speck on their horizon. Most of us know that compared to
many millions in the world, we look wealthy to them. The
call in the scriptures to the Christian community is to look
beyond ourselves and participate in God's economy in which
those who need...receive and those who have something to
give...give. When we realize how much we have is a gift, it
makes the giving easier.

■ ■ ■

Holy God, make us abundantly aware of our abundance and
our ability to give. Amen.

July 24

Mark 5:30-1,33-34
Immediately aware that power had gone forth from him,
Jesus turned about in the crowd and said, "Who touched my
clothes?" He looked around to see who had done it. But the
woman, knowing what had happened to her, came in fear
and trembling, fell down before him and told him the whole
truth. He said to her, "Daughter, your faith has made you
well; go in peace, and be healed of your disease. "

■ ■ ■

The beauty and the brilliance of Mark's Gospel is in the
economy of words to deliver oceans of meaning. Jesus had
the power to heal. The woman had the faith to believe that
just touching his clothes would help. In the midst of many
people pressing in on him, Jesus felt a single, needy touch.
The woman was bold enough to fall down before Jesus and
tell him the truth. Jesus gave her more than just the
healing of a disease, but an identity inside a relationship.
He called her "daughter." The power of what Jesus has to
offer the world transcends geography, common sense, time,
blood lines. We can dare to believe that a savior who walked
among a crowd of people thousands of years ago in a far
away country is still touching us today.

■ ■ ■

Precious Lord, take our hands and give us healing, hope,
and love. Amen.

July 25

Isaiah 55:10-11
For as the rain and the snow come down from heaven, and do not return there until they have watered the earth, making it bring forth and sprout, giving seed to the sower and bread to the eater, so shall my word be that goes out from my mouth; it shall not return to me empty, but it shall accomplish that which I purpose, and succeed in the thing for which I sent it.

■ ■ ■

After having become a homeowner with a lawn, I discovered the Zen-like state of being a "Lawn Worrier." When the rain does NOT "come down from heaven" and do its thing, then we have to figure out other ways to spread the water around. The water when it reaches the roots accomplishes its purpose. The Hebrews have an understanding of words that make them as tangible as water. Words go out of our mouths and have substance and purpose. The words born of God's Spirit within us when it reaches the roots of the hearers gives new life. Our words need the blessing of God's grace and our willingness to irrigate the lives of those around us with the words that makes us grow.

■ ■ ■

Rain upon us, Lord, that we might grow. Bless our thoughts and words with your life-giving purposes. Amen.

July 26

Psalm 65:4-6
Happy are they whom you choose and draw to your courts
to dwell there! They will be satisfied by the beauty of your
house, by the holiness of your temple. Awesome things will
you show us in your righteousness, O God of our salvation,
O Hope of all the ends of the earth and of the seas that are
far away.

■ ■ ■

My summer childhood days were spent exploring the wilderness of the next street over or the field "out back." Grandeur was lying in a field of daisies and Queen Anne's lace and watching the sun turn a drop of dew into a gem worthy of a jewelry store. Treasure was a Indian Head penny, a bottle cap, or a stone embedded with mica. Our future danced with visions of possibilities. The God of our salvation, the hope of all the ends of the earth continues to restore our sense of wonder by letting us know that we have only just begun to see how magnificent God is. The best is still yet to be. Until then, we are children just beginning to explore this amazing neighborhood.

■ ■ ■

Awesome God, restore in us a sense of wonder in all things
great and small that we might revel in your wild
imagination and find our wealth in you. Amen.

July 27

Romans 8:22-24
We know that the whole creation has been groaning in labor pains until now; and not only the creation, but we ourselves, who have the first fruits of the Spirit, groan inwardly while we wait for adoption, the redemption of our bodies. For in hope we were saved.

■　■　■

I am learning there is a difference between moving through our days "groaning" as the scriptures say or living our days hopefully and patiently. Both ways take a lot of energy. Patience is like a muscle that needs to be conditioned, nurtured, and flexed. It is something that when used regularly builds on itself, but patience like a muscle has limits - it can be overloaded, strained, pulled, torn. We can exercise patience when we know that the outcome will be worth the wait. God gives us hope that his purposes are being worked out - daily and eternally - even as we work out the muscle of our patience.

■　■　■

Holy God, may we be as patient with ourselves, one another, and you as you have been with us. Amen.

July 28

Ezekiel 2:4-5
The descendants are impudent and stubborn. I am sending you to them, and you shall say to them, "Thus says the Lord God," Whether they hear or refuse to hear (for they are a rebellious house), they shall know that there has been a prophet among them.

■ ■ ■

We all know stubborn when we see it in another person. We get frustrated that they may not let us get a word in edgewise. Their opinion or perspective seems totally unaltered or unaffected by anything we have to say. We always have to respect the freedom of adults to ignore us even when we have their best interest at heart. God chooses to treat us like adults even when we behave like children. God respects our freedom to ignore him. God, however, still insists on sending the message and the messengers to us on a regularly basis. We only have ourselves to blame when we don't face the truth. The God of grace continues to send the message that we can be forgiven, but we have to listen.

■ ■ ■

Holy God, may we recognize a hardened heart especially when we see it in ourselves. Amen.

July 29

Psalm 123:3-4
Have mercy upon us, O Lord, have mercy upon us, for we
have had more than enough of contempt. Our soul has had
more than its fill of the scorn of those who are at ease, of
the contempt of the proud.

■ ■ ■

How quickly we learn to look down on other people.
Children do it. Teenagers do it out loud with lethal prowess.
Adults do it but we are often smart enough to check our
condemnation at the door of our mouths, but then it sits as
a pile of refuse in our hearts. We are quick to identify those
with more than we have. More money, more time, more
family, more friends, more meaningful work, more health,
more talent, more intelligence. The wall between us is built
in the matter of seconds. And the wall will stand
permanently and effectively between us until we recognize
that building the wall has created nothing good. The
psalmist leads us to lift our eyes to God, confess that we
have had more than enough contempt, and beg for his
mercy. From the lap of his unwalled mercy, we gain a new
perspective of ourselves and one another.

■ ■ ■

Holy God, forgive us when we try to find our place in the
world by looking down on others. Help us to find our home
in you. Amen.

July 30

2 Corinthians 12:7b-10
Therefore, to keep me from being too elated, a thorn was
given me in the flesh, a messenger of Satan to torment me,
to keep me from being too elated. Three times I appealed to
the Lord about this, that it would leave me, but he said to
me, "My grace is sufficient for you, for power is made
perfect in weakness." So, I will boast all the more gladly of
my weaknesses, so that the power of Christ may dwell in
me. Therefore I am content with weaknesses, insults,
hardships, persecutions, and calamities for the sake of
Christ; for whenever I am weak, then I am strong.

■ ■ ■

On some rear view mirrors are the words "Objects in the
mirror are closer than they appear." Paul did some major
whining to the Lord in the midst of his struggle before he
came to realize that God's love for him was closer than it
appeared to be. It is often only in hindsight that we can see
how God has been faithful to us through the darkest
moments. We need reminders, not in our rear view, but
through the front window that God's grace is closer than it
appears. As the song goes, "Little ones to him belong, they
are weak but he is strong, yes, Jesus loves me."

■ ■ ■

In the midst of our pain and weariness, remind us, O Lord,
of how near you are. Amen.

July 31

John 2: 20
This temple has been under construction for forty-six years.

■　■　■

"Under Construction" is a sign that used to be seen exclusively at building sites or highways. Today it isn't unusual to see such a sign on the internet. Sometimes it implies caution. Mostly it means, "We are still working on this so be patient." Anyone would scoff at the notion of anything important being built swiftly. Here in John's Gospel they were talking about the temple in Jerusalem - where a Jew could come and know without a doubt that God was present. Jesus claimed he could rebuild it in three days and it isn't any wonder that few people believed him. Some came to understand what he was saying after his resurrection. In a few days, Jesus rose from the dead and constructed a ways and means of grace for the whole world. He dusted off his hands and threw away the "Under Construction" sign and we abide and thrive in state of grace what Jesus built in three days.

■　■　■

Almighty God, though our journey is incomplete we know our home is secure in you. Thanks be to God. Amen.

213

August 1

Psalm 85:10-11
Mercy and truth have met together; righteousness and
peace have kissed each other. Truth shall spring up from
the earth, and the righteous shall look down from heaven.

■ ■ ■

The summer is often a time of conventions, workshops, and gatherings for people who work for or are members of various organizations. They parade out the best speakers they can find. They entice the most renowned experts in the field to offer their wisdom. Imagine a convention where the keynote speakers are Mercy, Truth, Righteousness and Peace. Who would not want to be in the presence of such wisdom? Their speaking fees would be through the moon. While we amuse ourselves with the impossibility and the attractiveness of such a wild idea, we are invited to a meeting with Mercy, Truth, Righteousness, and Peace. The meeting begins with the words, "Let us pray...."

■ ■ ■

I will listen to you, O Lord, help me to believe what I hear and follow as you lead. Amen.

August 2

Ephesians 1:5-6
He destined us for adoption as his children through Jesus
Christ, according to the good pleasure of his will, to the
praise of his glorious grace that he freely bestowed on us in
the Beloved.

■　■　■

From his prison cell, Dietrich Bonhoeffer penned a poem in
which he asked, "Who am I?" He articulated what we all
have asked at some time in our lives. Are we the labels that
others put on us? Are we the same person today and
another one tomorrow? At any given time, we may define
ourselves as sinner or saint, weakling or hero, hypocrite or
moral pillar. The struggle of our identity lingers and mocks
us and let to our own devices will drive us to a brink of
insanity or apathy. Bonhoeffer ended his poem with a
statement of faith. "Who am I? They mock me, these lonely
questions of mine. Whoever I am, thou knowest, O God, I
am thine."

■　■　■

Whoever we are, thou knowest, O God, we are thine. Amen.

August 3

Mark 6:22-24

*When his daughter Herodias came in and danced, she
pleased Herod and his guests; and the king said to the girl,
"Ask me for whatever you wish, and I will give it." And he
solemnly swore to her, "Whatever you ask me, I will give
you, even half of my kingdom." She went out and said to her
mother, "What should I ask for?" She replied, "The head of
John the Baptizer."*

■ ■ ■

Not a pretty story. A head on a platter and ugly family
dynamics. The mother was trying to solve a politically
difficult situation for her husband who was too conflicted to
make a decision. The daughter was trying to please the
mother. In the end, John the Baptist - servant of the Lord
and the first proclaimer of the Kingdom of God in our midst
- was killed. Nothing about it feels good or right or true.
This seamy underbelly of family dysfunction and poor
leadership have enough power to silence the voice crying in
the wilderness, "Prepare the way of the Lord!" What we do
know is that as ugly as this story is, the Lord still came and
his Kingdom is now. Not even death can silence the voice of
God's good news.

■ ■ ■

Holy God, may we proclaim your kingdom today. Amen.

August 4

Jeremiah 23:3-4
Then I myself will gather the remnant of my flock out of all
the lands where I have driven them, and I will bring them
back to their fold, and they shall be fruitful and multiply. I
will raise up shepherds over them who will shepherd them,
and they shall not fear any longer, or be dismayed, nor shall
any be missing, says the Lord.

■　■　■

I talked with a couple whose daughter had run away from
home as a teenager and was well into her adult life now but
still missing. The couple hired detectives. There was some
indication that she was alive and working in another state,
but she resisted any attempt on their part to find her. She
chose to remain lost to them. The holes in the parents'
hearts were enormous and filled with guilt for what they
could have done or not done to have remained in a
relationship. God is aware of those we have driven away or
let drift away from connectedness to his community. We
cannot be responsible FOR one another but we can be
responsible TO one another. God intends to be our shepherd
and to find all who are lost. We are called to help by flexing
the muscle of grace and forgiveness with one another every
day.

■　■　■

Good Shepherd, watch over us and help us to be ever
mindful of one another. Amen.

217

August 5

Psalm 23:5-6
You spread a table before me in the presence of those who
trouble me; you have anointed my head with oil, and my
cup is running over. Surely your goodness and mercy shall
follow me all the days of my life, and I will dwell in the
house of the Lord forever.

■ ■ ■

I knew some folks who own a catering business. To stay in
business they need to make careful calculations about how
much food to offer for how many people. At the same time,
however, one of the practices they value is that no customer
ever says, "We didn't have enough food." More often than
not his customers say, "We had more than enough! It was
great!" We all know of some relative who would rather die
than for someone to walk away from their table still
hungry. This wonderful psalm continues to remind us of a
God who is overflowing in his abundant care for us even in
the midst of our deepest struggles. In our relationship with
God, we lack nothing and are caught in the overflow of love
and mercy.

■ ■ ■

Holy God, we hunger for justice, peace and love. You feed us
to overflowing. May we respond to your generous heart by
fighting hunger wherever we find it. Amen.

August 6

Ephesians 2:13-14
But now in Christ Jesus you who once were far off have been brought near by the blood of Christ. For he is our peace; in his flesh he has made both groups into one and has broken down the dividing wall, that is, the hostility between us.

■ ■ ■

In our relationships, we have issues about which we disagree. The disagreement creates a new pattern of contentious communication between us. The matter may be resolved but the pattern of hostility remains. It is not unlike siblings that are at war with one another constantly even though the topic of their disagreements changes. As my sister and brothers grew into adulthood, we barely knew how to communicate with one another and often resorted to adolescent teasing. We never allowed the relationship to grow up. Christ, our brother, intervenes and gives us an opportunity for peace and to find a different way to relate to one another.

■ ■ ■

Holy God, draw us close to your cross so that the distance between us fades away in the presence of your love. Amen.

August 7

Mark 6:31-32
He said to them, "Come away to a deserted place all by yourselves and rest a while." For many were coming and going, and they had no leisure even to eat. And they went away in the boat to a deserted place by themselves.

■ ■ ■

We all know those people who are able to catch a quick 10-20 minute naps during the day and wake up refreshed and raring to go. I am not one of those people. I do sleep well most nights but there are nights when I wish there was a way to turn off my brain (that didn't involve substance abuse!). Needing to be at leisure is important to the rhythm of our lives. Jesus recognized this for his disciples. The shores of their days were filling with crowds needing their time and attention. A short time in a boat provided a small oasis in which they could rest. In the blaze of overly busy, overly scheduled days, we may hear the voice of Jesus inviting us to "Come away." The world will catch up with us soon enough.

■ ■ ■

Lord God, in our restlessness, help us to find our rest in you. Amen.

August 8

John 1: 48
"Where did you get to know me?" Jesus answered, "I saw
you under the fig tree..."

■　■　■

One of the often repeated sentiments I hear during pre-marital counseling is that "He knows me. She knows what I am thinking. We can finish each other's sentences." In our most intimate relationships, trust is absolutely critical and fragile. Trust can be under girded with a deep knowledge that is sown with benevolent purposes. To be known by one who we do not know or trust can be unnerving. To enter into a relationship with Jesus, we encounter someone who knows us better than we do ourselves. If the fear of being discovered doesn't chase us away, we will find in Christ one whose motives are completely for us. To grow in the intimate knowledge of Jesus is to discover a loved one who enjoys filling in the blanks of our incomplete sentences.

■　■　■

Holy God, help us not to be afraid of your intimate
knowledge of who we are. Amen.

August 9

2 Kings 4:42, 44
A man came from Baal-shalishah, bringing food from the
first fruits to Elisha, the man of God; twenty loaves of
barley and fresh ears of grain in his sack. Elisha said, "Give
it to the people and let them eat." He set it before them,
they ate, and had some left, according to the word of the
Lord.

■ ■ ■

One of the good things about getting older (and there are
good things!) is that I have more stories I have witnessed of
God's faithfulness to me and others. Part of the legacy of
the Old Testament is watching the faith of the people of
Israel as they collect stories of a God who keeps his
promises. They do not pray just to the God of Abraham but
to the God of Abraham, Isaac, and Jacob...the God of King
David....and the God of the prophets like Elisha. Each had
their own testimony to the nature of God and the certainty
of his faithfulness. The food that was brought was not
enough to feed 100 people. God promised that it would be
enough and it was more than enough. In taking steps into a
fearful and unknown future, we are accompanied by the
witness of ancient prophets and our own memories of a God
who has never abandoned us.

■ ■ ■

Make us ever mindful, Lord, of the history of your people
and the future you have promised. Amen.

August 10

Psalm 145:18-19
The Lord is righteous in all his ways and loving in all his works. The Lord is near to those who call upon him, to all who call upon him faithfully.

■ ■ ■

I can still hear my mother's voice saying, "Debra, do you ever think before you send words flying out of your mouth?" I've gotten better about thinking before speaking but words still come out of my mouth that cause hurt. None of us could ever define ourselves as righteous in all our ways and loving in all our works. We are not much better than misbehaving school children when it comes to a bit of gossip especially the kind that serves no other purpose but to hurt people. We are even more dangerous when we think what we are doing is righteous. For the sake of love, we can try to think before we speak and act. We can ask ourselves, "What does love require?" But even our best intentions will sometimes falter and someone will be hurt. We, who cannot be wholly righteous or loving in our thoughts, words and deeds, are called to stand near to the Lord, confess our sins, and receive his mercy so that we can learn mercy day after day after day.

■ ■ ■

Guard our tongues, our thoughts, our deeds. Convict us of our sins and be merciful to us, O Lord. Amen.

223

August 11

Ephesians 3:18-19
I pray that you may have the power to comprehend, with all
the saints, what is the breadth and length and height and
depth, and to know the love of Christ that surpasses
knowledge, so that you may be filled with all the fullness of
God.

■ ■ ■

There are moments, sometimes just random flashes that
appear like butterflies or a patch of blue sky on a dark day.
They are moments when beauty or truth in the purest form
appears before us as if to say...this is what beauty really
looks like....this is how truth feels.....this is a glimpse of how
we will know one another and be known in the Kingdom of
Heaven. If we are not too consumed with the present
agenda, we will not miss the power of it to take our breath
away. We will look forever different at all that the day
holds before us. I saw a child the other day on the tiptoes of
becoming a teenager and beautiful beyond her years, full of
herself and full of the love that God has for her. As
Tennessee Williams once wrote, "Sometimes there is God so
quickly."

■ ■ ■

Holy God, you amaze us with your love. Don't ever stop.
Amen.

August 12

John 6:20-21
But he said to them, "It is I; do not be afraid." Then they
wanted to take him into the boat, and immediately the boat
reached the land toward which they were going.

■ ■ ■

And now for your trivia moment of the day: The word 'immediately' is used 83 times in the Bible and two-thirds of the occurrences are in the New Testament particularly in the Gospels. The stories of Jesus are filled with immediacy. The word revealed the urgency of the situation or it emphasized the miraculous nature of an event. The immediacies of our daily lives are almost always about urgency and rarely about miracles. The Gospel writers wanted us to live inside their experience as they walked with Jesus. There was something about him that was both urgent and miraculous. We are the object of both Christ's urgency to secure our salvation and the miracle of his sustaining grace.

■ ■ ■

Holy God, help us not to miss the miracles that surround us even as we move urgently through our days. Amen.

August 13

I Kings 19:11b-13

Now there was a great wind...but the Lord was not in the wind; and after the wind an earthquake, but the Lord was not in the earthquake; and after the earthquake a fire, but the Lord was not in the fire; and after the fire a sound of sheer silence. When Elijah heard it, he wrapped his face in his mantle and went out and stood at the entrance of the cave. Then there came a voice to him that said, "What are you doing here, Elijah?"

■ ■ ■

One summer I took a freighter across the Atlantic and back again. Freighter engines are constantly running and are rarely shut down except for major repairs. The thrum of the engines is a sound and a vibration one grows accustomed to hearing and feeling. One night, the generator failed and the engines stopped. The silence was like someone pounding me on the chest. It took my breath away. Elijah must have felt something like that after the whirlwind. Into the thundering silence, came the voice of the Lord to Elijah. In the midst of the din of our noisy lives, God creates the space for us to hear his voice. Sometimes it feels like someone pounding on our heart, wanting to get in.

■ ■ ■

Lord God, help us to turn our faces in your direction and lean our ears into your voice. Amen.

August 14

Luke 3:10-11
And the crowds asked him, "What then shall we do?" In reply, he said to them, "Whoever has two coats must share with anyone who has none; and whoever has food must do likewise."

■ ■ ■

There is a little book called the Penguin Principles: A survival guide for clergy. It is a book of wise and honest advice to help clergy be realistic about life in the parish so that they can endure the difficult times which always happen when people try to do anything together. One of the principles is that, at any given time, only about 5% of the people are working unselfishly - the rest are saying, "What's in it for me?" The individuals of that 5% change from day to day – even minute to minute. The challenge for clergy is accepting that. The even bigger challenge for clergy is trying to be one of those 5% as often as possible. But we don't ...we do slip. We spend our emotional energy thinking of only ourselves and trying to rest on, or worse yet, create our laurels. We don't bear good fruits when we are consumed with ourselves. The best of who God created us to be is when we turn ourselves inside out and consider the needs of those around us.

■ ■ ■

Forgive us, Lord, our self absorption and generate in us good things for others. Amen.

227

August 15

Romans 10:14-15
But how are they to call on one in whom they have not
believed? And how are they to believe in one of whom they
have never heard? And how are they to hear without
someone to proclaim him? And how are they to proclaim
him unless they are sent? As it is written, "How beautiful
are the feet of those who bring good news!"

■ ■ ■

Proclamation is a word that evokes images of pulpits and preachers. Certainly proclamation is done in those places by those people, but proclamation can happen and does happen in much more intimate moments. When we pull the Gospel through our own soul and out for the sake of another person, we offer the story of Christ with the footprints of our own tale of sin and forgiveness. There is no greater gift that we can give than to stand inside our own redeemed feet and give a gift of hope.

■ ■ ■

Lord God, thank you for the privilege of being bearers of the good news. Amen.

August 16

Matthew 14:22,24

Jesus made the disciples get into the boat and go on ahead to the other side of the Sea of Galilee... he went up the mountain by himself to pray. When evening came, he was there alone, but by this time the boat, battered by the waves, was far from the land, for the wind was against them. And early in the morning he came walking toward them on the sea.

■ ■ ■

Separation anxiety. I've seen it in the quaking bodies of toddlers being dropped off for day care. I've witnessed it in the quivering phone call of an adolescent home alone searching for a parent or in a spouse padding about aimlessly. I was surprised by the twinge of melancholy I felt after experiencing the first birthday since my mother's death. Disciples were sent away on a boat without Jesus and without knowing how or when Jesus would join them. Jesus spent the night alone waiting to take a morning walk to meet his friends. If Jesus felt any separation anxiety, he spent the time praying and perhaps sleeping. The disciples spent the night worrying. I have determined it is not a bad way to deal with the aloneness....to pray hard and sleep well.

■ ■ ■

Holy God, chase our anxiety away and grant us a day of tenderness and a night of peace. Amen.

August 17

Isaiah 56:1,6-7
Thus says the Lord: Maintain justice, and do what is right,
for soon my salvation will come, and my deliverance be
revealed. And the foreigners who join themselves to the
Lord, to minister to him, to love the name of the Lord, and
to be his servants, all who keep the Sabbath, and do not
profane it, and hold fast my covenant - these I will bring to
my holy mountain, and make them joyful in my house of
prayer; their burnt offerings and their sacrifices will be
accepted on my altar; for my house shall be called a house
of prayer for all peoples.

■ ■ ■

Doing what is right not as easy as it sounds. There is the
problem of our sinful eyes. There is the problem of our
reluctance to be bold. There is the problem of our fear.
There is the problem with our arrogance. I have had and
still have those times in my life when I chafe at the idea of
being anyone's servant and when obedience to anything or
anyone besides my own conscience is repugnant. And yet, I
know that some of the most peaceful moments of my life
have been doing chores that only love required. One could
do quite well in life being a servant in the house of the
Lord. The right thing is costly but it never costs us a place
in God's house.

■ ■ ■

Lord God, receive the sacrifice of our contrite hearts. Amen.

August 18

Psalm 67:1-2
May God be merciful to us and bless us, show us the light of his countenance, and come to us. Let your ways be known upon the earth, your saving health among all nations.

■ ■ ■

"Please don't give up on me." It is the tearful plea of a person who knows that he or she has made mistakes and doesn't deserve love or loyalty. It is also the plea of one who knows that love and grace are as essential as breathing. The worst thing God could do to us is simply to walk away and remain hidden from us. The best thing is that, despite our sin, weakness and shame, God makes himself available and known to us. The cross is God's response to our plea - God will go to the ends of the earth and the bottom of the pit to keep us close.

■ ■ ■

Don't give up on us, Lord. We do not deserve your devotion but without your grace, we cannot live. Amen.

231

August 19

Romans 11:29
For the gifts and the calling of God are irrevocable.

■ ■ ■

This verse has been the guardian at the door every time I have ever wanted to run screaming from the responsibilities of being a follower of Jesus Christ. "You can run but you can't hide" it seems to taunt. We have all been given gifts and we have all received in our baptism the call to serve. Neither the gifts nor the call goes away. They may languish in the attic of our carelessness, but they remain. The gift vibrates with the need to be used. The calling relentlessly speaks to us no matter how far we wander. Strangely enough, when we have stopped our running and pouting and flailing after empty dreams, this verse truly is good news.

■ ■ ■

Lord, help us to recognize our gifts, embrace them and prepare ourselves to be obedient to your calling for the sake of the world. Amen.

August 20

Matthew 15:10-11
Jesus called the crowd to him and said to them, "Listen and understand; it is not what goes into the mouth that defiles a person, but it is what comes out of the mouth that defiles."

■ ■ ■

Gary Chapman in his book "Five Love Languages" outlines that there are five identifiable ways in which we receive the message that we are loved. The five methods are words, acts of service, gifts, quality time, and touch. We all have a preferred method of receiving that message. Our preference may be so strong that even though the message might be delivered in other ways, we still walk away thinking that we are not loved. It will come as no surprise that words are important to me. Over the years, I have come to appreciate even more how words can cause deep hurt, tarnish our reputation, and destroy our credibility. I have also learned that the opposite is powerfully true - words can lift a person up and surround them with the fragrance of hope. The word "Jesus" is a love letter to the whole world.

■ ■ ■

Lord, speak to us that we may speak in words that do not destroy, but communicate in a variety of ways that we are greatly loved. Amen.

233

August 21

Isaiah 51:1-2
Listen to me, you that pursue righteousness, you that seek
the Lord. Look to the rock from which you were hewn, and
to the quarry from which you were dug. Look to Abraham
your father and to Sarah who bore you; for he was but one
when I called him, but I blessed him and made him many.

■ ■ ■

There is the old story about the parent who thought he
could keep a child occupied for a long time by chopping up a
picture of the world to make a puzzle for the child to put
together. The child finished the task quickly and when the
parent asked how he did it, the child said, "There was a
picture of a person on the back and once I put the person
together, the world came easy." God is building his new
kingdom one person at a time. As we focus on our Lord and
understand our roots, we are healed in our sinfulness and
given the power to choose righteousness. From one person
comes a story of God's faithfulness and mercy. From one
cross comes God's salvation for us. From each of us comes a
story so wonderful that it has the power of changing the
lives of many.

■ ■ ■

Lord God, the complexity of healing our world is
overwhelming. Help us to see that one person at a time,
hope is contagious. Amen.

August 22

Psalm 138: 2-3
I will bow down toward your holy temple and praise your name, because of your love and faithfulness; for you have glorified your name and your word above all things.

■ ■ ■

Our culture is riddled with voices that cry out for individual freedom, rights, and entitlement. The idea of bowing down is a rare, lonely, and often misunderstood cry in this modern wilderness. The issues with which we struggle as Christians seem to grow more complex every day and are fueled by those of us who are very sure that they have the truth. Sorting out the complexity involves the simple act of resting in the One whose grace in the face of our sinfulness brings us to our knees. What brings us together is not a like mind but a contrite heart. What empowers us is not our corner on the truth but a call to obedient servanthood.

■ ■ ■

Holy God, grant your stiff-necked people the ability to bend at the heart so that we might worship and serve you well. Amen.

August 23

Romans 12:1-2
I appeal to you therefore, brothers and sisters, by the
mercies of God, to present your bodies as a living sacrifice,
holy and acceptable to God, which is your spiritual worship.
Do not be conformed to this world, but be transformed by
the renewing of your minds, so that you may discern what
is the will of God - what is good and acceptable and perfect.

■ ■ ■

"What is the will of God?" I wish I had a quarter for every time I have heard that question. We are a people called, gathered, chosen, redeemed and sent. We are still a sinful people and even as we are called and sent, we must sort through the fog of our own humanity, our own basic cravings, our own distorted mindsets. To present ourselves to God is to offer ourselves up for refurbishing. We confess our flawed and broken nature and ask for what only God can do in transforming us into his first thought of us. As we are transformed, so the clarity of God's will shines through the fog. Too often, we ask for clarity before we are willing to make an investment in the answer. In sacrifice for the sake of others, we learn how God's will works.

■ ■ ■

Holy God, receive the sacrifice of our broken hearts and weak spirits. Forgive us our sin and re-make us into the best idea you ever had and still have for us. Amen.

236

August 24

Matthew 16:15-16
He said to them, "But who do you say that I am?" Simon
Peter answered, "You are the Messiah, the Son of the living
God."

■ ■ ■

It was time for the disciples of Jesus to speak out loud what
they had all been thinking, hoping, suspecting, even
fearing. It was time to say that Jesus was not just any
footnote in the history of the people of God. This Jesus was
all history, all that was, and all that is to come in one being
both human and divine. We dance around issues. We play
nice. We have political correctness down to an art form.
There are just some times when we need to blurt out the
truth without shame or fear or embarrassment. There are
times when we must say who we believe Jesus is. Perhaps
the time is today for us to speak of what we have seen and
heard.

■ ■ ■

God, stir up the courage within us to blurt out the truth
about you as our Savior, Lord and source of all that is good.
Amen.

August 25

Jeremiah 15:15-16
O Lord, you know; remember me and visit me, and bring down retribution for me on my persecutors. In your forbearance do not take me away; know that on your account I suffer insult. Your words were found, and I ate them, and your words became to me a joy and the delight of my heart; for I am called by your name, O Lord, God of hosts.

■ ■ ■

Rather high on my list of "Jobs I Don't Envy" is Old Testament prophet. They were called to an extremely thankless job that often did not bear any fruit - if any - during their lifetime. They were given stern messages from God to deliver to the people, and we all know what we do to the messenger of bad news. Jeremiah's prayer life was riddled with his own sense of inadequacy and failure, paranoia and not a little whining. The power of his witness for us is in the fact that he always trusted in the One who listened to his whining relentlessly. The power of God's grace is seen in that God never gave up on his whiney prophet or the people to whom he sent him.

■ ■ ■

Lord God, we have a thousand things to do with no time or help or gratitude. But Lord, you listen to your whiney people and bless us anyway. Thank you! Amen.

August 26

Psalm 26:1-3
Give judgment for me, O Lord, for I have lived with
integrity; I have trusted in the Lord and have not faltered.
Test me, O Lord, and try me; examine my heart and my
mind. For your love is before my eyes; I have walked
faithfully with you. I have not sat with the worthless, not do
I consort with the deceitful.

■ ■ ■

Integrity - it is one of my favorite words though I don't
know if I can be so bold as the psalmist to say I have always
lived with integrity. To be a person of integrity means that
our words, actions, and choices match our most cherished
beliefs and values. The opposite is compartmentalization -
when we behave one way but talk another. It takes great
integrity not to be affected by a culture that is riddled with
cruelty and selfishness. God offers his love that we can see,
taste, and touch so that we can walk faithfully. It is not a
bad idea that the psalmist gives us to return to the Lord
once in a while to ask, "How am I doin', Lord?"

■ ■ ■

Lord God, may we see your love, walk in faith, repel evil
and act on what we believe to be true about you. May we
not be afraid to ask you for help. Amen.

August 27

Romans 12:9-13
Let love be genuine; hate what is evil, hold fast to what is good; love one another with mutual affection; outdo one another in showing honor. Do not lag in zeal, be ardent in spirit, serve the Lord. Rejoice in hope, be patient in suffering, persevere in prayer. Contribute to the needs of the saints; extend hospitality to strangers.

■ ■ ■

Paul always moves from theological to practical in his letters. His words to the Romans sound like the litany of a parent to a child as they shoulder their school bags and head out the door. As we are sent into the world, the voice we hear over our shoulder loves us well and knows that we bear within us the power to carry love into another person's life. That love is born of God's heart and brings God's redemption into the world. Such is the magnitude of what can be accomplished in offering a prayer, a hand, a moment of understanding, an open heart. Have a good day, child of God, you are greatly loved - spread it around.

■ ■ ■

Holy and merciful God, you have attended to our needs, listened to our cries so now send us forth into this day with bags packed with the gifts of love and tenderness you have given to us that we might give to others. Amen.

August 28

Matthew 16:24
Then Jesus told his disciples, "If any want to become my
followers, let them deny themselves and take up their cross
and follow me.

■ ■ ■

There was a time in my life when what I most wanted for myself was invisibility. It is not that I wanted to disappear. If anything, I wanted desperately to belong, to be included, but my presence was messy and seemed to be disruptive and burdensome. I wanted to be with others without causing a mess. The denial of self and the journey of a cross bearer is not a call to invisibility or the erasing of our personality. We cannot save ourselves or keep our own messiness from leaking out in our relationships. If anything, we are called to be more completely who we are - sinners in need of forgiveness - clinging intentionally to the One who keeps our messiness from condemning us and destroying the people we love. The world falls through our fingers if we try to cling to anything else.

■ ■ ■

We trust you, Lord. Amen.

August 29

Ezekiel 33:10-11
Now you, mortal, say to the house of Israel, Thus you have said: "Our transgressions and our sins weigh upon us, and we waste away because of them; how then can we live?" Say to them, As I live, says the Lord God, I have no pleasure in the death of the wicked, but that the wicked turn from their ways and live; turn back, turn back from your evil ways; for why will you die, O house of Israel?

■ ■ ■

One of my favorite lines of scripture which is also our worship liturgy as the Gospel is about be read is - "To whom shall we go? You have the words of eternal life." In our arrogance and stubborn self-sufficiency we move through our lives and turn our relationship with God into a pleasant accessory or emergency management equipment. God has a good reason to be weary of our fickled nature. God does not, however, let death - the consequence of our sinfulness - have the last word. God doesn't weary of sending voices to us saying, "Stop your foolishness and turn to me."

■ ■ ■

Lord God, help us not to deny our sinful nature and to rely on your grace. Amen.

August 30

■ ■ ■

Teach me. Those words do not happen authentically without being preceded by a few character-building honest moments. They imply there is something we don't know and need to be taught. Admitting we don't know something seems to be getting harder and harder these days. To speak them also implies that the request is being made to someone whose teaching we trust. Unfortunately, trust is in rather short supply too. We can try to teach ourselves but that would be about as foolish as doing our own dental work. Imagine if we entered each day asking God to teach us. In that request, we admit our limitations, profess our trust, and open ourselves to a host of amazing new discoveries.

■ ■ ■

Lord God, teach us this day to open our hearts and minds to your will and trust your abiding lessons. Amen.

August 31

Romans 13:10-12
Love does no wrong to a neighbor; therefore, love is the
fulfilling of the law. Besides this, you know what time it is,
how it is now the moment for you to wake from sleep. For
salvation is nearer to us now than when we became
believers; the night is far gone, the day is near. Let us then
lay aside the works of darkness and put on the armor of
light.

■ ■ ■

When we witness a catastrophic event like a natural disaster, there are many who can and do respond and many more who don't know what to do. We see suffering and we want to do something to help. To watch the spreading catastrophe bleed and strangle the hope out of people's lives without knowing quite yet how to help is sobering. The time will come for us to assist our neighbors. The time will come when there will be something we can do. At that moment, may we not be so consumed with our own needs that we are asleep to the needs of others. The time will come for us to don armor of light. What we can do is prepare our hearts to be awake and ready to love God's people with our whole heart.

■ ■ ■

Holy God, in every step we take today may we take inventory of the blessings we have and the blessings we have to share. Amen.

September 1

I Kings 19:7-8
The angel of the Lord came a second time, touched him, and said, "Get up and eat, otherwise the journey will be too much for you." He got up, and ate and drank; then he went in the strength of that food forty days and forty nights to Horeb the mount of God.

■ ■ ■

A week at camp is always a good time with the exception of dealing with the Texas heat. Best way to deal with the heat is to drink alot of water. We were given our own water bottles by the camp staff. Water was readily available. Getting our kids to fill those bottles and drink more water than they were used to drinking in a day was a challenge. Some weren't eating and drinking enough to balance their activity level. They were the ones in and out of the nurse's cabin and the ones who were dragging through the day and not having a very good time at all. Elijah wanted to sit under a tree and die, but God gave him something to eat and drink. It is a basic lesson for us all in our care for one another. We must not ignore the fundAmen.tal needs so that we can know the abundance of life.

■ ■ ■

Holy God, may we take in the water and the food that you provide for us so that we may have energy for the journey. May we use that energy to make food and water happen for one another. Amen.

245

September 2

Psalm 34:5-6
Look upon him and be radiant, and let not your faces be
ashamed. I called in my affliction, and the Lord heard me
and saved me from all my troubles.

■ ■ ■

One of the finest Christian men I ever knew was a pastor at
a nearby church when I began ordained ministry. He took
me under his professional wing and mentored me in my
fledgling years. When one is immersed in seminary books
for years, it is easy to forget that grace is more than a
theological concept. It is a way of life. My pastoral mentor
was a man acquainted with his own sins, fully aware of his
limping soul, but even more fully alive in the grace he knew
in Jesus Christ. He didn't have an arrogant bone in his
body and lived in a state of grace better than anyone I have
ever known and taught me how to live that way too. When
we are aware of our own sinfulness and aware of God's love
and mercy....there is no room for arrogance....ever.

■ ■ ■

Lord God, convict us of our sinfulness and uphold us with
your grace that we might move mercifully through our
days. Amen.

September 3

Ephesians 4:29
Let no evil talk come out of your mouths, but only what is
useful for building up, as there is need, so that your words
may give grace to those who hear.

■ ■ ■

Oh, how I wish it were as easy as being on the bridge of the
Starship Enterprise. The captain issues a command to his
first officer and says, "Number One, Make it so!" We have to
labor intentionally and conscientiously to manage our
temper. We have a tendency to speak ill of one another, to
believe the worst, to tear one another down, to twist the
truth, or to plant seeds of outright lies. At the same time,
we are just as responsible to work diligently at what we
hear from others so not to become a part of the toxic system
that spreads evil viruses. We need our own "Thought, Word,
and Deed Purification Plant" so that "garbage in" does not
equal "garbage out." Would that we could remember to
filter everything we think and hear through the cross of
Christ.....make it so, Lord, make it so.

■ ■ ■

Forgive us, Lord, for grieving your Spirit and create a clean
heart in us so that we may build up the Body of Christ
today. Amen.

September 4

John 6:35
Jesus said to them, "I am the bread of life. Whoever comes
to me will never be hungry, and whoever believes in me will
never be thirsty."

■ ■ ■

The Gospel of John is filled with the great "I am" statements of Jesus. In the Old Testament , God referred to himself as "Yahweh" which means "I am." Jesus said I am light, bread, shepherd, vine, gate, way, truth, resurrection, and life. Our generation experiences the most interdependence that any culture has ever known. We are more personally disconnected from the land and more dependent on farmers, truckers, manufacturers, processors, distributors, and retailers to get the grain from the field to become bread on our table. At the same time, we still insist on our independence. We push and shove and jockey for position in our relationships with family and work. Jesus cuts through the din of our own posturing to declare the true source of all that we are, all that we need, and all that we own. He is the source of our lives and all our lives flow from him.

■ ■ ■

Holy God, with each morsel of bread, may we taste the goodness of your ever present care. Amen.

248

September 5

John 2:5
His mother said to the servants, "Do whatever he tells you."

■ ■ ■

Mary, the mother of Jesus, did not have to take the "faith car" out for a test drive. She already knew how faith handles the road. Mary was the first believer in Jesus. No one knew better in the early days of his ministry just who Jesus truly was. She could rest on her laurels as the first. She had already served God well in believing, risking, bearing, laboring, and nurturing. Even still, she continued to follow and believe. At the wedding at Cana, she stepped out boldly in faith and was consequently rebuked for pushing God's timing. Mary did not shrink away nor disagree with Jesus' rebuke. She did confidently instruct the servants to listen to Jesus. She had to accept that what he chose to do and when it was his call to make. Mary, as the first believer, does help to show us all how to walk with faith and to point others to Jesus.

■ ■ ■

Lord God, thank you for Mary and for all who help us to walk in faith. Amen.

September 6

Psalm 34:9-11
Fear the Lord, you that are his saints, for those who fear
him lack nothing. The young lions lack and suffer hunger,
but those who seek the Lord lack nothing that is good.
Come, children, and listen to me; I will teach you the fear of
the Lord.

■ ■ ■

One college community I lived in years ago had a train track that went over the end of a dam. There was little ground on either side of the tracks and the drop off was a severe one to jagged rocks below. Periodically, a college student would try to walk the tracks, get caught in the path of an on-coming train, and tragically fall to their death. A few years would pass before it would ever happen again because the story had created enough precaution to avoid it. But when there was a new crop of students who had no memory of such fear, another student took a fall. We teach our children to have a healthy respect for the Lord. We don't do this to make them tremble through their days. We do this because we love them so much.

■ ■ ■

Holy God, make us bold to teach our children the most valuable lessons we know - that you are bigger than we will ever be and filled with more love for us than we can imagine. Amen.

September 7

Ephesians 5:18b-20
Be filled with the Spirit, as you sing psalms and hymns and
spiritual songs among yourselves, singing and making
melody to the Lord in your hearts, giving thanks to God the
Father at all times and for everything in the name of our
Lord Jesus Christ.

■ ■ ■

"With rings on her fingers and bells on her toes, she shall have music wherever she goes." The modern version of the rhyme would more likely be..."With phones in our ears and tunes on our pods, we shall have music wherever we trod." I love that music has become so marvelously available to us in so many electronic mediums. There is still no replacement for the live music of a grand piano, a pipe organ, an acoustic guitar, a human voice, a choir, a symphony, or a band. There is the priceless sound of a loved one singing a hymn as you hold the book together. Sometimes at worship I stop singing a hymn for a phrase or two just to listen to the people sing. As the saying goes, "to sing is to pray twice." It is good to gather for worship to sing, listen, praise, and pray!

■ ■ ■

Holy God, surround us with the sound of music so that we may hear what we can accomplish together when we are pointed in your direction. Amen.

September 8

John 6:51-53
"I am the living bread that came down from heaven.
Whoever eats of this bread will live forever; and the bread
that I will give for the life of the world is my flesh." The
Jews then disputed among themselves, saying, "How can
this man give us flesh to eat?" So Jesus said to them, "Very
truly, I tell you, unless you eat the flesh of the Son of Man
and drink his blood, you have no life in you.

■ ■ ■

From our point of view of the Gospel story, we can see the short-sightedness of the Jews toward Jesus. It is our own short-sightedness that gives us trouble. How often we are quick to judge. We set our minds. We dig in our heels and look for confirmation of our own judgment. The worse the relationship, the deeper we dig in and the more energy we use. The Jews, in their defense, were absolutely certain that they were right and that Jesus was a heretic of a giant order. "What if...." is one of my favorite phrases because it is the crack under the door that lets the light through and invites the possibility of a new way of seeing, especially a new way of seeing one another. What if we saw one another first, last, and always as bearers of the Good News of Jesus, children of God, fellows members of the Body of Christ?

■ ■ ■

Holy God, repair our vision so that we might see Christ alive in the world and in one another. Amen.

September 9

John 1: 38
When Jesus turned and saw them following, he said to
them, "What are you looking for?"

■ ■ ■

The end of the Gospel of John is rich with the long farewell discourses of Jesus. The beginning, however, starts with simple statements and questions. We take no journey unless we know why we are going. When we look to Jesus and consider following, it is in response to a deep need in our lives that we may not have even dared to articulate. Not even the disciples could answer that question directly. They asked Jesus where he was staying and Jesus said, "Come and see." It would be easy to say Jesus is the answer but it takes away our responsibility to explore the question of what we are looking for. The relationship with Jesus is sown in the soil of our hunger for relief from the brokenness of our own making and for wholeness beyond our ability to create. Even to spend time with Jesus while we work out the questions is holy time.

■ ■ ■

Holy God, be patient with us as we sort through the confusion and begin to see more clearly. Amen.

September 10

Joshua 24:15
Now if you are unwilling to serve the Lord, choose this day
whom you will serve, whether the gods your ancestors
served in the region beyond the River or the gods of the
Amorites in whose land you are living; but as for me and
my household, we will serve the Lord."

■ ■ ■

We have developed a mall-mentality as a people. Shopping malls give us readily available, easily accessible choices. We want choices....lots of them. And we want to be able to return purchases if we change our minds. We want choices and we want to be able to change our minds and make other choices. We even want the option of not choosing at all. Sometimes sitting on a fence for too long only gives us splinters. When it comes to the big choices, who we will serve....who will be the god of our lives....we need to choose. We need to choose today and every day whom we will serve. We also need to witness to our choice. As for me and my house, we will serve the Lord.

■ ■ ■

Holy God, you chose us and have stood firm in that choice. Help us this day and always to choose you. Amen.

September 11

John 1: 23
I am the voice of one crying out in the wilderness, 'Make
straight the way of the Lord.

■ ■ ■

Living alone, I have the luxury of decorating as I wish and
living comfortably among my own messes. When faced with
the possibility of guests in my house, I look at my living
quarters differently. What do the pictures on my walls say
of me? What messes in particular do I want to hide away?
What would be an obstacle to my guest's comfort? To
prepare the way of the Lord means we must first recognize
our messes for what they are. It also means to acknowledge
that being in God's presence is so special that we would not
want anything to get in the way of our time together. Our
self-consciousness of our own sin is what most stands
between us and God. When we receive forgiveness we have
the freedom to see outside ourselves, especially the guest at
the door.

■ ■ ■

Almighty God, grant us the courage to clean up our lives
and enjoy your presence. Amen.

September 12

Psalm 34:18-20
The Lord is near to the brokenhearted and will save those
whose spirits are crushed. Many are the troubles of the
righteous, but the Lord will deliver him out of them all. He
will keep safe all his bones; not one of them shall be broken.

■ ■ ■

I have visited slave quarters that were preserved since the
post-Civil war period. I have visited the dormitories that
housed the people imprisoned in concentration camps
during World War II. The witness of those who have been
unjustly treated cries out even in those hollow rooms that
stand as monuments to our human cruelty. Through the
rubble of their despair come voices that seem incredulous
for they speak of hope and sing of God. In spite of all the
evidence to the contrary, many of them believed in the
power of God to overcome. From time to time, we stand in
the rubble of much smaller piles of injustice and we look to
the saints to teach us the songs of hope.

■ ■ ■

Holy God, deliver us, keep us safe, we turn our lives to you.
Amen.

September 13

Ephesians 6:10-11
Be strong in the Lord and in the strength of his power. Put on the whole armor of God, so that you may be able to stand against the wiles of the devil.

■ ■ ■

We have grown rather sophisticated in our culture in regards to evil. We have fashioned evil into the grand landscape of comic books and mystic legends. The ancient heroes and sagas live on because we want to believe that evil is easily recognizable and just as easily vanquished. Evil exists and though it certainly doesn't parade around in public with a name tag, it still surfaces like a sink hole to undermine our lives. It hovers around the most vulnerable. The best offense is a good defense. The saying works in football and in works against the enemy within us and around us. We have some impressive defensive armor and the weapon of God's Word to strengthen our resolve.

■ ■ ■

Holy God, protect us from our own naiveté about the nature of evil, protect us, and help us find our strength in you. Amen.

September 14

John 6:67-68
So Jesus asked the twelve, "Do you also wish to go away?"
Simon Peter answered him, "Lord, to whom can we go? You
have the words of eternal life.

■ ■ ■

It was difficult for even the closest of Jesus' disciples to hear that God was God and they were not God. Human beings like control. Either we want to make the decisions ourselves or we want to be the one who decides who will decide. Letting go is not in our nature. But Jesus gives us an ultimatum that we do not want to hear. Either we live in the knowledge of God's sovereignty in our lives or we choose to turn our backs and live the lie that we are in control. There are plenty of times we get angry at God and we don't like God's way of doing things. We may even pout and stomp out the door but when we do, we dangle our toes at the abyss of darkness. Over our shoulders are the lights of home. It is worth eating a little crow to walk back in.

■ ■ ■

Lord, to whom can we go? You have the words of eternal life. We have come to believe and know that you are the Holy One of God. Amen.

September 15

Deuteronomy 4:7,9
For what other great nation has a god so near to it as the
Lord our God is whenever we call to him? But take care and
watch yourselves closely, so as neither to forget the things
that your eyes have seen nor let them slip from your mind
all the days of your life; make them known to your children
and your children's children.

■ ■ ■

Bette Midler sings some awesome songs. She has a unique and powerful voice. There is one song of hers, though, that I really hate. The chorus goes, "God is watching us from a distance." What a colossal lie! My experience of God has been one in which he uses every imaginable vehicle for communication - audio, visual, sensory. God is, in fact, not distanced and not just watching. God's most potent method of communication is Jesus himself. Just as Jesus came and lived among us so now the Spirit of the Living God is a breath away, the sound of our own heart beating in our ears, and a vibration of truth. It would take a lot of work to shut God out. God will find away. It is easier to listen to God and use our eyes and hands to know God than to ignore him.

■ ■ ■

Holy God, thank you for being just a breath away. Amen.

September 16

Psalm 15:1-2
Lord, who may dwell in your tabernacle? Who may abide
upon your holy hill? Whoever leads a blameless life and
does what is right, who speaks the truth from his heart

■ ■ ■

"Whoever leads a blameless life....." I can't speak for anyone but myself but, Lord knows that would rule me out of being able to tramp around on God's holy hill. When we are all honest, no one is blameless. Incredibly, God still wants us on his hill and so he sent his Son to die for us. We sin. Through Christ we can minister to that sin without trampling the sinner. We don't deserve the view from the hill, but it is ours nonetheless. Thanks be to God.

■ ■ ■

Holy God, convict us of our sin and help us to enjoy the view from the heights of your mercy. Amen.

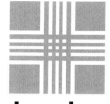

September 17

James 1:19-22
You must understand this, my beloved: let everyone be
quick to listen, slow to speak, slow to anger; for your anger
does not produce God's righteousness. Therefore rid
yourselves of all sordidness and rank growth of wickedness,
and welcome with meekness the implanted word that has
the power to save your souls.

■ ■ ■

The Greek word translated as meekness has inadequate translations in English. It does not mean docile rather it speaks more of a perfect blend of excessive anger and excessive angerlessness. It is the energy of anger without the wickedness of it. We are to take in the Word of God that has been given to us. We are not to let it lay dormant on the surface of who we are but take it in with a controlled energy. We are to be humble enough to learn and embrace the discipline of learning. A person of integrity is not passive but actively listening, waiting for the right time and the right words, and has their anger under control. They integrate God's Word into every fiber of their being and what comes out is the stuff that lifts up the Kingdom.

■ ■ ■

Thank you, Lord, for your life-changing Word. Give us the courage and strength to pull it through our souls for the sake of the world. Amen.

261

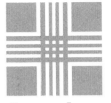

September 18

Mark 7:14-15
Then he called the crowd again and said to them, "Listen to me, all of you, and understand: there is nothing outside of a person that by going in can defile, but the things that come out are what defile."

■ ■ ■

I knew a woman who used to say that it was all right to spell curse words out loud but not to say them. She was a vigorous speller. We usually failed to hear anything she had to say while we were busy forming the words in our head that she was spelling. What we say.....be it curse words or unkindness or lies.....reflects powerfully upon our character. The Jewish people of Jesus' day had a very tightly defined definition of clean living. It had much to do with their dietary laws. Jesus expands the definition of clean living to include how we speak, what we say and do as an indication of the cleanliness of our souls.

■ ■ ■

Create in me a clean heart, O God, and renew a right spirit within me. Amen.

September 19

Matthew 18:19-20
Again, truly I tell you, if two of you agree on earth about
anything you ask, it will be done for you by my Father in
heaven. For where two or three are gathered in my name, I
am there among them.

■ ■ ■

There was a science fiction movie called "Sphere." The plot
was a bit complicated, but in the end the remaining
characters discovered that they had been given a gift to
make their thoughts real - for good or for ill. After a series
of missteps and tragedy, they decided human beings
weren't ready for such a gift and decided together to use the
power one last time to forget how to use it. Sometimes I
think that we as Christians have forgotten the power of the
Body of Christ gathered in Christ's name. To be a
community that bears the name of Christ has the power
and strength to defy the forces at work in the world. The
power is greatest when we remember who we are.

■ ■ ■

Lord, your children wander homeless and cry for bread and
hope. Help us know how to use the power you have given us
as your gathered people. Amen.

September 20

Genesis 50:17-18
*Say to Joseph: I beg you, forgive the crime of your brothers
and the wrong they did in harming you.' Now therefore
please forgive the crime of the servants of the God of your
father." Joseph wept when they spoke to him. Then his
brothers also wept, fell down before him, and said, "We are
here as your slaves."*

■ ■ ■

"Helicopter parent" is a phrase I have heard that refers to
parents who hover too close to their children in order to
fight their battles for them. In their defense, it is because
the children are so greatly valued. We want no harm to
come to them physically or emotionally. Sometimes it just
isn't a good idea to be flung into the deep end of the pool
and left there. However, the time comes when boys become
men and girls become women and they must know how to
fight their own battles and stand on their own two feet. The
sons of Israel could no longer count on their father to bail
them out of trouble or use his power to manipulate what
they wanted to achieve. They were left with the option to
start to grow up by learning to get on their knees. That is
an important part of growing up - to know one's limitations.

■ ■ ■

Lord God, forgive us our sins, receive us as your sons and
daughters. Amen.

September 21

Philippians 4:7
And the peace of God, which surpasses all understanding,
will guard your hearts and your minds in Christ Jesus.

■　■　■

I had a dream last night in which two strangers who were up to no good came into my house while I was there. The dream was a jumble of nonsense as most dreams are. I found myself trying to talk with them about how they got through a locked door. As it turned out the door was porous and the strangers literally walked through the door. I remembered thinking in the dream, I need to post a guard. We cannot live our lives AND guard our hearts and minds at the same time. We need help. We need to be able to rest knowing that we are protected from evil. Paul reminds us that God will, in fact, post a guard on our hearts that we might find the strength we need to face each day with hope and grace.

■　■　■

Holy God, thank you for standing watch over us while we grow in your grace. Amen.

September 22

Romans 14:7-8
We do not live to ourselves, and we do not die to ourselves. If we live, we live to the Lord, and if we die, we die to the Lord; so then, whether we live or whether we die, we are the Lord's.

■ ■ ■

The word underneath my picture in the high school yearbook says, "loner." It was not a source of pride for me only the result of a young life caught up in the tug of war between needing to be alone and away from the din of the world, and yet wanting desperately to be a part of the world without bringing it more empty noise. The Gospel of God shows a better way to live and a better way to love. We cannot remove ourselves from humanity neither can we enter into it without complicating it. And so, we look to Jesus. We trust his mercy and grace. We live and die and find joy in knowing and believing that we are never alone, even when we try to be. We are eternally God's.

■ ■ ■

God of Grace, free us from the burdens of our sin and grant us responsibilities that we can shoulder together with you. Amen.

September 23

Matthew 18:21-22
Peter came and said to [Jesus], "Lord, if any member of the church sins against me, how often should I forgive? As many as seven times?" Jesus said to him, "Not seven times, but, I tell you, seventy-seven times."

■ ■ ■

We tend to think of ourselves as forgiving people. Forgiving people to their face challenges us to our core. We may say we forgive people who don't even know that they offended us because we don't want to deal with facing them. That is not how forgiveness works at its best. That only puts our relationships at a distance. When the Matthew 18 process is honored then confession and forgiveness take place. The relationship can be restored. It will last until the next time we offend one another and we confess and forgive over and over and over again. Hopefully we have enough of a learning curve that we are not making the same offense over and over again. We give one another the time and the forgiveness to get some elevation in that curve. Grace gives us time and hope. We need a lifetime of time and an ocean of hope. Jesus knew that about us and loved us nonetheless.

■ ■ ■

Lord, we give you thanks for those people in our lives who do not give up on us. Help us to forgive quickly and love relentlessly. Amen.

September 24

Jonah 3:10-4:2a
When God saw that [the people of Ninevah] did, how they
turned from their evil ways, God changed his mind about
the calamity that he had said he would bring upon them;
and he did not do it. But this was very displeasing to Jonah,
and he became angry. He prayed to the Lord...

■ ■ ■

When I get angry, I do a variety of things depending on the social setting. I clench my teeth. I cut off the conversation. I hang up the phone. I leave the room. Over the years, I would hope that my response has become more socially mature, but all the responses involve the cessation of talking on my part. Jonah had a relatively new relationship with God, and yet demonstrated a remarkable trust in venting his anger at the one who made him angry. Jonah was confused and frustrated by God's change of plans and so he hammered back. God responds to Jonah's anger by teaching him something about his nature. Keeping the channels of communication open is one of those no-brainer maxims to live by and yet we regularly cut off our communication with God when we are too busy, too angry, too confused. Those are the times when God most wants to hear from us.

■ ■ ■

Precious Lord, help us to be quick to pray especially when we are angry and confused. Amen.

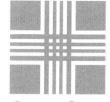

September 25

Psalm 145:8
The Lord is gracious and full of compassion, slow to anger and of great kindness.

■ ■ ■

Those words feel like the comfort of clean sheets and a soft pillow at the end of a busy day. At the same time, they feel like a punch in the chest. Oh, how we need God's grace and patience with our behavior about which he is within his rights to be angry. Oh, how badly we mirror that Godly character in how we relate to others - especially those closest to us. Where God's patience seems limitless, ours is short-fused. Inside the comfort of God's amazing grace, we find the space to vent, to ease the quaking of our hearts, to find the temper that we lost. Inside that grace, we rarely find neat solutions - only a reason not to give up on one another. Some days, that is everything.

■ ■ ■

Holy God, grant me the grace to love as you love - one day at a time - forever. Amen.

September 26

Philippians 1:27-28a
Only, live your life in a manner worthy of the gospel of
Christ, so that , whether I come and see you or am absent
and hear about you, I will know that you are standing firm
in one spirit, striving side by side with one mind for the
faith of the gospel, and are in no way intimidated by your
opponents.

■ ■ ■

Our courtrooms are daily filled with those who are seeking to know who is to blame for crimes committed or mistakes made. Even in hindsight, we are not always able to identify quickly and clearly how, when, and who made mistakes. The guilty party may be identified. What, if anything can be done to prevent the same mistake from happening in the future is not always so clear. Being able to identify "the enemy" - the opponent to a life lived worthy of the Gospel of Christ is not always easy as it sounds. It is definitely not a life meant to be lived alone. We need one another's faith and vision especially when we cannot recognize when we are being compromised, lead astray, or fooled. The call to know what we believe and who believes it and to strive together in that one faith is a call that needs constant renewal and vigilance.

■ ■ ■

Holy God, when we have lost our way, send us a sister or a brother to steady our step. Amen.

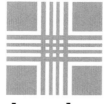

September 27

Matthew 20:8
When evening came, the owner of the vineyard said to his
manager, 'Call the laborers and give them their pay,
beginning with the last and then going to the first.

■ ■ ■

In my experience as a pastor, I have heard many highly personal and confidential pieces of information about people's lives. It still amuses me that the most intimate information that people rarely talk about is the actual amount of their salaries. Oh, sure - we know the going rate for a plumber, a professional baseball player, a teacher - so we can guess, but it still not something we like to talk about. Our heads immediately go into a metaphysical form of mathematics where we try to determine if what we do is equal to the dollar figure of what someone else receives doing some other kind of work. We are told in the kingdom of heaven we will be treated well. We will get more than we deserve. God is the Boss. The Boss is very, very generous. In the Kingdom of Heaven, salary won't be an issue.

■ ■ ■

Lord God, may your kingdom come and your will be done on earth as it is in heaven. Amen.

September 28

Ezekiel 18:31-32
Cast away from you all the transgressions that you have
committed against me, and get yourselves a new heart and
a new spirit! Why will you die, O house of Israel? For I have
no pleasure in the death of anyone, says the Lord God.
Turn, then, and live.

■ ■ ■

"Gottado" It is a phrase that is part of my running mental
stream in the morning. I gottado this and I gottado that. It
is always a mix of obligations like a bill payment, house or
car maintenance, work-related projects, and people to
contact. It always includes changing habits that will make
for a healthier life. When one is only accountable to oneself
for life-giving and even life-saving behaviors, there is a
tendency to let those things get swallowed up in the tidal
wave of other "Gottados." Transgressions against God take
on many forms. Most insidious among them is living our
lives thinking that we are accountable to no one. To do and
be the best of what God created us to be means to stop
doing the stupid things. We will be freer to turn to God and
live.

■ ■ ■

Lord, we lift up our ever-growing list of things we ought
and should do. Help us to choose the things that make for
life. Amen.

September 29

Psalm 25:5-6
Remember, O Lord, your compassion and love, for they are
from everlasting. Remember not the sins of my youth and
my transgressions; remember me according to your love and
for the sake of your goodness, O Lord. Gracious and upright
is the Lord

■ ■ ■

I would do just about anything to keep myself from
intentionally causing my friends undue pain or discomfort.
I feel the same about my relationship with God. But I cause
problems. I don't intend to fling myself into the sin, but, in
retrospect, that is exactly what it looks like. No brain
engaged. No hint of concern about consequences. I just
screw up. We fling ourselves at the mercy of our friends,
family, and God to forgive us. If we are truly blessed, we
can learn from the ones who choose not to give up on us.
Inside that mercy, we discover even more motivation to love
well because we have been treated with honesty and grace.

■ ■ ■

Lord, help us to learn to love as we have been loved. Amen.

September 30

Philippians 2:10-11
So that at the name of Jesus every knee should bend, in heaven and on earth and under the earth, and every tongue should confess that Jesus Christ is Lord, to the glory of God the Father.

■ ■ ■

When a hurricane bears down on us, there is absolutely nothing that can be done to stop it. No government agency or branch of the military can plan an offensive strategy. We can only respect its strength, get the heck out of its way, pray, and hope we are all safe and sound to clean up afterwards. When it comes to the storm of our turbulent lives, we tend to believe we are more powerful than we are. God's call to servanthood and obedience points us to the cross. It beckons us to bow in the presence of the greatest power in heaven and on earth - the power of God's love for us in that he sent his own son to die that we might live.

■ ■ ■

Lord God, we acknowledge your power in our lives. Amen.

October 1

Matthew 21:23
When Jesus entered the temple, the chief priests and the elders of the people came to him as he was teaching, and said, "By what authority are you doing these things, and who gave you this authority?"

■ ■ ■

I have had a boatload of dental work done over the past few years. I am caught by surprise at how much I stare at my dentist's credentials framed on the wall. I am even more surprised by how relieved I am that they are from a recognizable university and look authentic. I want to know that the person with the sharp tools in my mouth knows what he is doing. We can't blame the temple leaders for questioning Jesus' credentials. However, authenticity doesn't always come to us in wall frames of well-earned documents. Sometimes it comes to us in the person of God's own son.

■ ■ ■

Lord God, grant us grace to accept our vulnerability and trust in your authority. Amen.

October 2

John 11:19
And many of the Jews had come to Martha and Mary to console them about their brother.

■ ■ ■

"I don't know what to say." Those words are probably among the most frequently uttered at a funeral. In the presence of someone in emotional pain, we are often at a loss for words. We know from our own experience or just instinctively that whatever words we say may fall uselessly to the floor like petals from a wilting flower. At best, we try to stand on the edge of their ocean of pain with our toes in the water and try to feel their numbing cold. At worst, we keep our distance and get swallowed up in our own guilt. The most powerful consolation we can offer most often is simply our presence. Our grace-filled presence, our willingness to wade into the icy waters to stand with one another in the ocean of hurt can touch a broken heart. The Jews gathered to console Mary and Martha in their pain. Jesus chose to come close to their pain and to ours. He chose to wade into the ocean of human sin and misery. In choosing to come close to one another in Christ's name, we will find the redemption that is available to us all.

■ ■ ■

Lord, may we know the consolation of your love and extend that loving presence to others. Amen.

October 3

Psalm 80:12-14
Why have you broken down its wall, so that all who pass by
pluck off its grapes? The wild boar of the forest has ravaged
it, the beasts of the field have grazed upon it. Turn now, O
God of hosts, look down from heaven; behold and tend this
vine; preserve what your right hand has planted.

■ ■ ■

The scriptures are filled with illustrations evoked by the earth. Agricultural images were daily and pervasive occurrences. It makes me wonder what the psalms would sound like today if they were written in the environment of computers, cell phones, and cars. Does our distance from the earthly work tend to imagine a God more distant? The purpose of the scripture is to help us know what is important for us to know about the nature of God. God speaks in small voices and in the whirlwind. God creates the world in a word and tends to sparrows. Whether our vision is myopic or far-sighted, we may be compelled to ask "So where is God?" God is in the question that we never seem to stop asking. There is faith even in a doubtful question.

■ ■ ■

Holy God, help us to experience your closeness through the images of our daily lives so that we might breathe as you breathe and serve as you serve. Amen.

277

October 4

Philippians 3:10-11
I want to know Christ and the power of his resurrection and the sharing of his sufferings by becoming like him in his death, if somehow I may attain the resurrection from the dead.

■ ■ ■

When we hang around people long enough and we admire these people, we allow ourselves to be influenced by them. We start to use phrases that they use. We listen more openly to their opinions. We take to heart more deeply their comments, even their off-handed ones. We allow them inside us and we are changed. As we come to know Christ through his word and sacraments and through one another, we are given the opportunity to allow him to influence us and change our way of seeing and living. We are given the opportunity every day for others to see and know Christ through us.

■ ■ ■

Lord, may those we love and those we encounter through the day know Jesus because of us today. Amen.

October 5

Matthew 21:42-43
Jesus said to them, "Have you never read in the scriptures:
'The stone that the builders rejected has become the
cornerstone; this was the Lord's doing, and it is amazing in
our eyes'? Therefore I tell you, the kingdom of God will be
taken away from you and given to a people that produces
the fruits of the kingdom.

■ ■ ■

We get into a lot of trouble when we try to own anything - people or things. Things depreciate. Things need to be used carefully. Things cost money. People can't be owned. We can't make ourselves a part of anyone else's life. We are, however, given the gift of things and relationships. With them, we are called to produce the good stuff of which the kingdom is made. When we try to do anything else, such as assuming ownership, we fall on our face. When God picks us up, dusts us off, and forgives us....there is always a sense that he is muttering under his breath...."I told you about this once....in a parable."

■ ■ ■

Lord God, help us to acknowledge that everything and everyone in our lives is a gift from you. Amen.

October 6

John 11: 35-36
Jesus began to weep. So the Jews said, "See how he loved him.

■ ■ ■

It was a question asked as a discussion starter at a youth group meeting. "When was the last time you cried and for what reason?" It is a good question. It gives us a clue about what is important to us. Tears can roll for a variety of reasons, but one important reason is because of someone for whom we feel compassion. Jesus loved Lazarus. Those who were watching could see it. But Jesus also hated death. The one place in scripture where we see Christ's tears is the place where his two great passions collide head-on. Jesus could do something about his love for Lazarus by raising him from the dead. Lazarus would live to die another day and because of that Jesus took his other passion- his hatred of death to the cross. Tears continue to be shed by the people of God but because of Christ's passion, we can believe that one day the crying will end.

■ ■ ■

Lord God, receive our tears and thank you for loving us so passionately. Amen.

October 7

Isaiah 35:4-6
Say to those who are of a fearful heart, "Be strong, do not fear! Here is your God. He will come with vengeance, with terrible recompense. He will come and save you." Then the eyes of the blind shall be opened, and the ears of the deaf unstopped; then the lame shall leap like a deer, and the tongue of the speechless sing for joy.

■ ■ ■

I received a wooden cross in the mail from a friend with a card that read, "Courage doesn't always roar. Sometimes courage is the quiet voice at the end of the day saying, 'I will try again tomorrow.' We can make some educated guesses about the conditions the Hebrew people were encountering at the time Isaiah wrote these words. The words transcend time and circumstance. We all know inside our daily journey, our own private fears and the presence of enemies and the niggling doubt of our inadequacy. In the cross of Christ we are given, not the power to be right, but we are given tomorrow and the day after that....and the day after that. We are given the grace to keep trying because God's day will come and we will be in that day free and unafraid.

■ ■ ■

Holy God, grant us the courage to rely on your grace and face our fears every day. Amen.

October 8

Psalm 146:4-5
Happy are they who have the God of Jacob for their help,
whose hope is in the Lord their God; who made heaven and
earth, the seas, and all that is in them; who keeps his
promise forever

■ ■ ■

"Help, Lord." It is a short prayer but a perfect one. Even though we are encouraged to bring our concerns to God we often grow weary of the asking or don't know how to pray or what to pray for. The cry for help is one that prophets and kings have uttered for centuries. The God of Jacob has not ignored these cries. The issue becomes less about how that help will come and more about from whom the help comes. It is the Lord. It is our very big God who helps.

■ ■ ■

God of our salvation, we crawl into the lap of your grace and find our hope in you. Amen.

October 9

James 2:15-17
If a brother or sister is naked and lacks daily food, and one of you says to them, "Go in peace; keep warm and eat your fill, " and yet you do not supply their bodily needs, what is the good of that? So faith by itself, if it has no works, is dead.

■ ■ ■

Love sweats.

■ ■ ■

Lord God, your Son saved the world through his faith in you and his work on the cross. May we extend our thanks by making love work. Amen.

October 10

Mark 7:25-30
Now the woman was a Gentile, of Syrophoenician origin.
She begged him to cast the demon out of her daughter. He
said to her, "Let the children be fed first, for it is not fair to
take the children's food and throw it to the dogs." But she
answered him, "Sir, even the dogs under the table eat the
children's crumbs."

■ ■ ■

The landing strip for Jesus' entry into human history was built on the footpath of the people of Israel. His proclamation of the Good News was naturally to the Hebrew people. A woman, however, desperate and falling at his feet and begging for the life of her daughter was still first, a Gentile. He didn't have to speak to her at all. Jesus did choose to speak to her and he spoke to her as a Jewish man of the day would to a Gentile woman. The woman did not argue with him so much as she fully embraced the social label of "dog" because a crumb from his table for the sake of her daughter was worth the humiliation. Jesus saw beyond this woman's earthly labels and saw the beginnings of a right relationship with God - faith and humility.

■ ■ ■

Lord God, help us not to be so proud that we refuse to bow, so stubborn we refuse to ask, or so doubtful we refuse to believe. Amen.

October 11

Isaiah 50:4
The Lord God has given me the tongue of a teacher, that I may know how to sustain the weary with a word. Morning by morning he wakens - wakens my ear to listen as those who are taught.

■ ■ ■

Less than a century ago, a goat-herder looking for a lost goat threw a rock into a cave and heard something shatter. What he found were large clay pots containing ancient scrolls. The discovery came to be known as the Dead Sea Scrolls which included the largest, oldest, complete version of the book of Isaiah found to date. A treasure in an earthen vessel indeed. God through the ages has given us everything we needed to know in order to be God's people. Teaching and learning are at the heartbeat of what it means to be God's people. We are given the ears to hear. We are wakened in the morning by the whisper of his grace. We are given the tongue to speak of what we have seen and heard. We are a treasure in an earthen vessel to be a treasure for an earthen vessel.

■ ■ ■

Holy God, awaken in us the words that you whispered to us throughout our lives so that we might speak. Amen.

October 12

I Thessalonians 2:7b
But we were gentle among you, like a nurse tenderly caring
for her own children.

■ ■ ■

I worked with a couple of women who are relatively short in height but giant in stature. They are both mothers and have nursing degrees. Around people in need or hurting either physically or emotionally, they are the living definition of tenderness. With their own families they are steel magnolias. Their spouses and children know undeniably that they are loved, but they also know intimately the toughness of their character. We all know plenty of people who either bluster with noisy opinions or cut people with a thoughtless word. There are others who are so consumed with themselves that they are magnets for attention. But gentle souls do exist. They move through their days with a mother's attentiveness and a nurse's care. The ones who endure are often those whose strength of character is sustained by a faith in God who is tough with our sins and tender with our sorrows. Giants still walk the earth today in the form of those who love us with a soft touch and a firm hand.

■ ■ ■

Precious Lord, give us the wisdom to know when and how to be tender and tough. Amen.

October 13

James 3:8-9
But no one can tame the tongue - a restless evil, full of
deadly poison. With it we bless the Lord and Father, and
with it we curse those who are made in the likeness of God.

■ ■ ■

James doesn't pull any punches. He managed in a few words to reach through centuries with God's Word right now and take us all collectively to the woodshed. Sometimes being a part of a family means that we have to remember the rules of the house and to hold ourselves accountable. That means confessing when we unleash ugly words or set in motion gossip with ill intent. It means forgiving when we are on the ugly end of those words. Sometimes it means simply holding our tongue. On a good day, it means blessing God's people as richly and as lovingly as we have been blessed.

■ ■ ■

Lord God, we bless you and may the words of our mouths and meditation of our hearts bring honor and glory to you and all of your creation. Amen.

October 14

Mark 8:27
Jesus went on with his disciples to the villages of Caesarea
Philippi; and on the way he asked his disciples, "Who do
people say that I am?"

■ ■ ■

In the constant motion of today's family schedules, I have often thought that the dining room table should be on the endangered species list. The forlorn piece of furniture should be marked for extinction by tightly packed events in the day that allow for little time for sitting and talking. However, I have noticed that these conversations still happen but more on the fly and that good parenting is still happening, but it may be happening in transit. The challenge for the parent is being able to think fast on one's feet to seize the opportunity for "teaching moments." Jesus and his disciples were busy people, constantly in motion and yet profound teaching moments occurred that shaped their life of discipleship forever. May we be so keenly aware of those moments to teach and to learn about the grace and love of God.

■ ■ ■

Holy God, keep moving with us and ask us the questions that make us learn, think, and grow. Amen.

October 15

Jeremiah 11: 18-20
It was the Lord who made it known to me, and I knew; then you showed me their evil deeds. But I was like a gentle lamb led to the slaughter. And I did not know it was against me that they devised schemes, saying, "Let us destroy the tree with its fruit, let us cut him off from the land of the living, so that his name will no longer be remembered!" But you, O Lord of hosts, who judge righteously, who try the heart and the mind, let me see your retribution upon them, for to you I have committed my cause.

■　■　■

You gotta love Old Testament prophets....well, somebody's got to love them. They had one of the worst job descriptions in the world - "Go speak God's word to people who don't want to hear it." They were riddled with a deep sense of inadequacy and self-doubt. And just nobody liked them. One thing that they did have was the gift of a profound, intimate, eternal relationship with God. Jeremiah whined alot in his ministry. He complained. BUT...and there was always a BUT.....he knew who he was, who he was not, and he knew the righteousness of the One who had called him into service. And that was always enough.

■　■　■

Holy God, help us to see that there is nothing more important than being known by you. Amen.

289

October 16

Psalm 54:4
Behold, God is my helper; it is the Lord who sustains my life.

■ ■ ■

The cop shows on TV always lift up the value of the partner relationship. Going into a dangerous situation, it is absolutely necessary that one cop trust the other to watch their back. We walk everyday into the pitfalls and through the mine field of the dangers of life. We need to know that someone has our back. Simply put, God's got our back. We are to move with courage and faithfulness.

■ ■ ■

Holy God, protect us and guide us as we live and breathe. Amen.

October 17

James 3:13,18
Who is wise and understanding among you? Show by your
good life that your works are done with gentleness born of
wisdom. And a harvest of righteousness is sown in peace for
those who make peace.

■　■　■

One of the cherished parts of life at Texas A&M University
is the Aggie ring. It is a symbol of having completed many
courses, having been a part of one of the largest universities
in the country, and a sign for current and former students
of belonging to one another. The rings, when they are new,
are gold and shiny with crisp edges showing the seal of the
university. The older ones are rounded and smooth in spots
showing the results of years of wear. My own personal
experience has been that when we are open to life, our
edges gets worn off and there is, if we are willing to learn,
an opportunity to be a gentle presence, full of mercy. The
Spirit of the living God can be made known for the sake of
others when we make for peace.

■　■　■

God of Wisdom, blow your gentle spirit across our rough
edges so that we may serve you with a quiet mind. Amen.

October 18

Mark 9:33-34
Then they came to Capernaum; and when he was in the
house he asked them, "What were you arguing about on the
way?" But they were silent, for on the way they had argued
with one another who was the greatest."

■ ■ ■

The disciples didn't want to tell Jesus what they were arguing about because they knew in their guts that Jesus was going to take them to task to for it. Inside the community of Christ, we are just as likely to behave badly as outside of it. Jesus grabs us all by the ears and lifts us up on our toes so that we might hear that he expects better of us. He continues to love us through our wrangling but nevertheless sets a standard for our life together. The standard is that we put the needs of others before ourselves.

■ ■ ■

Holy God, may we learn to listen, love and serve one another to honor you. Amen.

October 19

Numbers 11:27-29
And a young man ran and told Moses, "Eldad and Medad
are prophesying in the camp." And Joshua son of Nun, the
assistant of Moses, one of his chosen men, said, "My lord
Moses, stop them!" But Moses said to him, "Are you jealous
for my sake? Would that all the Lord's people were
prophets, and that the Lord would put his spirit on them!"

■ ■ ■

One of the things I love about my church - both the
congregational and denominational expression of it - is that
it is a church of the baptized. The organizational authority
rests not in a bureaucracy or hierarchy where some have
more power than others but in each individual baptized
member. We do not promote "group think" where all are
expected to think the same way. What unifies us and makes
certain that we are still able to move together is the Spirit
of the living God. God is able to work out his purposes
through the most foolish and the most wise among us so
that his will is done. We are blessed to be bearers of that
spirit.

■ ■ ■

Breathe your Spirit upon us, O Lord, that we might use our
uniqueness for the sake of our common mission to serve
your Gospel. Amen.

October 20

Psalm 19: 14
Let the words of my mouth and the meditation of my heart
be acceptable in your sight, O Lord, my strength and my
redeemer.

■ ■ ■

I can still hear my mother's voice say, "Think before you speak!" My tendency to blurt out what is on my mind has gotten me in trouble on more than one occasion. Would that we had a little divine filtration system separating out the poisons and asking the right questions before we said a word. But the need for a clean heart goes even deeper to include the thoughts that roll around in our heads and fester and disease the soul. We can offer up our words and thoughts to a gracious God who washes us clean, checks behind the ears, and makes us more acceptable than we deserve.

■ ■ ■

Holy God, create in us a clean heart and renew a right spirit within us. Amen.

October 21

James 5:19-20
My brothers and sisters, if anyone among you wanders from the truth and is brought back by another, you should know that whoever brings back a sinner from wandering will save the sinner's soul from death and will cover a multitude of sins.

■　■　■

I remember Martin Sheen, the screen actor, speaking from the experience of his son's battle with drug addiction. He said with unbridled passion, "Do whatever you need to do to get between your children and drugs." Drugs mask the truth. That is their job. It is what they were invented to do. We invent other ways to mask the truth that are not so easily recognized. We need help to see the truth and to hear it ringing again inside our soul. When a brother or a sister speaks a lie, about themselves or another, we are to show them another way.

■　■　■

Lord, speak to us that we may believe the truth and speak it. Amen.

October 22

Isaiah 25:8-9
Then the Lord God will wipe away the tears from all faces,
and the disgrace of his people he will take away from all the
earth, for the Lord has spoken. It will be said on that day,
Lo this is our God; we have waited for him, so that he might
save us. This is the Lord for whom we have waited; let us be
glad and rejoice in his salvation.

■ ■ ■

When I was about 9 years old, I had a small newspaper route of about 30 customers. I was responsible for collecting the money and paying the newspaper company. Collecting money each week was not normally a problem, but I had disagreement with one customer about the correct amount due. I felt like I had the weight of the world on my shoulders. I thought I was right, but this person disgraced me in my youth. I still remember how low I felt and how long the walk home was that day. We are laid low by our sins and the judgment of others. We look for someone to help us or we give up on the idea of any help coming. A day spent waiting with hope versus a day spent hopeless and helpless is an easy choice. We wait with hope for the One who has always kept his promises.

■ ■ ■

Come, Lord Jesus, as we bear our burdens and wait with hope. Amen.

October 23

Psalm 23:1-3
The Lord is my shepherd; I shall not be in want. He makes me lie down in green pastures and leads me beside still waters. He revives my soul and guides me along right pathways for his name's sake.

■ ■ ■

If I wanted to spend the money, I could have a personal trainer, a life coach, and a financial planner. These people hold us accountable, cheer us on, challenge our slovenly behavior, and focus us on a goal. They ask the right questions and steer us away from our own stupidity. There is something in us that recognizes our need for a shepherd, but also is repulsed by it. We like our independence and we don't know who we could trust so thoroughly and sublimely with our lives. The Lord is the fulfillment of our deepest yearning - to be free, safe, and loved.

■ ■ ■

Holy God, help me to hear your voice in a noisy day. Help me to see your green pastures amid work and walls. Help me to find the stillness that my soul needs for the journey ahead. Help me not to resist your shepherding love. Amen.

October 24

Philippians 4:8
Finally, beloved, whatever is true, whatever is honorable,
whatever is just, whatever is pure, whatever is pleasing,
whatever is commendable, if there is any excellence and if
there is anything worthy of praise, think about these
things.

■ ■ ■

Yesterday I was walking on one side of a street and needed to cross to the other side. I was about to cross but decided to walk further until a car passed. Since it didn't pass as quickly as I had expected I looked over my shoulder at the car. The driver had slowed down expecting me to cross. When I turned to look at the car, he slammed on his brakes, and starting screaming at me, "Well, make up your mind, you !@#$@*." I crossed the street. Though I was sorry for my part in his confusion - I didn't feel like I deserved his rage. He diminished me. And it took the length of a city block to dust him off my soul. Truth and honor and purity don't rise to the surface with the velocity of anger. They need someone looking for them and opening a door. The word of the Lord is one which coaxes out the best of who we are in the image of God.

■ ■ ■

Lord, this day may we welcome truth and honor and purity into our day so that we may be the blessing for others. Amen.

298

October 25

Matthew 22:8-10
Then he said to his slave, "The wedding is ready, but those invited were not worthy. Go therefore into the main streets, and invite everyone you find to the wedding banquet'."
Those slaves went out into the streets and gathered all whom they found, both good and bad; so the wedding hall was filled with guests.

■ ■ ■

Several years ago, a large sorority was feeling the shock of the violent murder of one of their sisters. As a campus minister, I had been asked to come and speak with the women about how best they might care for one another in these sad days. I walked into a splendid and meticulously decorated room filled with fantastically dressed young women. I was out of my league and woefully underdressed to the point of shame. My taste in clothes has always been comfort over fashion. As unworthy as I was in my scruffiness, I was warmly greeted and was treated with respect and gratitude. The purpose of my presence far exceeded social propriety. We may feel unworthy to be in the halls of a King, but the invitation bestows on us a nobility. And the honor of the King's service gives us the comfort of belonging.

■ ■ ■

Lord, this is your world and your party. Thank you for your invitation. Amen.

October 26

Isaiah 45:4
For the sake of my servant Jacob, and Israel my chosen, I
call you by your name

■ ■ ■

When I see a headline about the latest Hollywood romance,
I shake my head wondering "who really cares?" I was born
around the time when Debbie Reynolds and Eddie Fisher
were the hot Hollywood item. "Debbie" became a rather
popular name for baby girls including me. I grew up
surrounded by dozens of people with my name. I decided to
go by "Deb" to be bold and different (hear the note of
sarcasm). That the Lord knows me by my name and seeks
for me to know him changes the sound and the power of my
name completely, as it does for all of us. To be known by
name by the Master of the Universe is to be subject to God's
authority and at the same time, made unique in all the
world.

■ ■ ■

Lord, in this day may we seek your face, your voice, and
your will and hear the special music of our own name
claimed by yours. Amen.

October 27

Psalm 96:11-13
Let the heavens be glad, and let the earth rejoice; let the
sea roar, and all that fills it; let the field exult, and
everything in it. Then shall all the trees of the forest sing
for joy before the LORD; for he is coming, for he is coming
to judge the earth. He will judge the world with
righteousness, and the peoples with his truth.

■ ■ ■

When headlines are marked with stories of hurricanes or earthquakes, it seems like the earth is groaning and restless. Birds scatter through the skies randomly when they know something big is coming. We don't spend much time thinking about Christ coming again, but there have been moments of global turmoil when I have thought, "Are you getting our attention, Lord?" It is not ours to know the hour of his coming. It is, however, an important part of what it means to be a faithful Christian to lean into a window from time to time, pressing our noses to it hoping that something wonderful is near.

■ ■ ■

Come, Lord Jesus, and bring the truth with you so that we may see it at last and live. Amen.

October 28

I Thessalonians 1:2-3
We always give thanks to God for all of you and mention
you in our prayers, constantly remembering before our God
and Father your work of faith and labor of love and
steadfastness of hope in our Lord Jesus Christ.

■ ■ ■

It isn't any surprise that Fortune 500 companies with the best employee satisfaction ratings are those who are attentive to their workers and reward their efforts beyond the paycheck. Even Paul, the champion of grace, understood that faith is sometimes work. Love is sometimes labor and hope is sometimes a physical effort. We work hard at the important things and rest at the end of the day in the hands of his grace knowing that our work is not what saves us. We live for and rest in the scarred hands of our Savior.

■ ■ ■

Today, O Lord, receive the work of our faith, our love, and our hope as a gift to you who loves us so well. Amen.

October 29

Matthew 22:15-16
The Pharisees went and plotted to entrap Jesus in what he said. So they sent their disciples to him, along with the Herodians, saying, "Teacher, we know that you are sincere, and teach the way of God in accordance with truth, and show deference to no one; for you do not regard people with partiality."

■ ■ ■

The Pharisees were not maniacally evil people. They were folks entrusted with a service to the faith community to interpret God's law. They were the Torah police. Especially in this time of the people of Israel, there were no kings, prophets, judges, or a messiah that they could see to guide them. The Pharisees and chief priests kept people focused and kept the faith from being diluted in a disassembled period of history. They attacked Jesus like a computer protection program going after a virus. They thought it was their job. They had stared at every word of scriptures so closely they had forgotten about looking for a messiah. The great tragedy of the Pharisees is that they didn't know the truth when it was staring them in the face. One can hardly blame them. The truth often hurts, but we can live with such a hurt.

■ ■ ■

Lord God, take the logs out of the eyes of our hearts and help us to see your love and grace everyday. Amen.

October 30

Leviticus 19:17-18
You shall not hate in your heart anyone of your kin; you
shall reprove your neighbor, or you will incur guilt yourself.
You shall not take vengeance or bear a grudge against any
of your people, but you shall love your neighbor as yourself:
I am the Lord.

■ ■ ■

I once owned a puppy that never got accustomed to being left alone on Sunday mornings. It had this uncanny ability to leave shredded bits of some important item by the door. One morning she pulled a Bible off my shelf and ate the entire book of Leviticus and a few Psalms. I kept the Bible for years because I didn't think I would miss Leviticus that much. But the book known primarily for its long lists of law codes does serve a purpose. It makes plain and succinct how we are, as God's people, to treat one another. Even though it is easier said than done, the law of love does not go away just because it is not easy. The Lord shows us how it can be done.

■ ■ ■

Holy God, help us not to chafe against your rules. May we be gentle neighbors. Amen.

October 31

Psalm 90:12
So teach us to count our days that we may gain a wise heart.

■ ■ ■

A man once told me that after you hit the age of 40 every day after that is gravy and he lived that way too. He enjoyed every day as best as he could. Another person told me the same thing about 50 and another about 60. We do tend to be a little better about counting our days when the ones we have left don't require a lot of math. But to do such counting leads to a wise heart - that is something we can still offer to one another no matter the condition of our bodies. We can offer wisdom cradled in love and delivered into the hands of those who spend their days unaware of the bigness of God and the preciousness of life.

■ ■ ■

Grant us, O Lord, a wise heart so that we can be honest about our shortcomings and love one another with the truth. Amen.

November 1

Psalm 34:8-9
Taste and see that the Lord is good; happy are they who trust in him! Fear the Lord, you that are his saints, for those who fear him lack nothing.

■ ■ ■

Welcome to sainthood! Today is All Saints Day. It happens to be my baptismal anniversary. I became a saint this day and I didn't do a thing to earn it nor have I done anything since then to earn it. We may chafe at the idea of being a saint, but we are nonetheless. Perhaps we have become so accustomed to our sinfulness, we don't want the responsibility of sainthood. Our sainthood comes to us as a gift of God - not as anything that we do. It isn't a cause for boasting because we didn't earn it, but it is cause for celebration because it is just so good. We ride on the shoulders of all the saints who have come before us. We rejoice that even knowing they have died, they will be at the party too.

■ ■ ■

Holy God, we praise your name and join with the hosts of heaven rejoicing in our sainthood and your amazing grace. Amen.

November 2

Matthew 22:37-39
He said to him, "'You shall love the Lord your God with all your heart, and with all your soul, and with all your mind." This is the greatest and first commandment. And a second is like it: "You shall love your neighbor as yourself."

■ ■ ■

Marketing experts tell us that we have to hear messages repeatedly, often over 14 times, before the information of the message actually starts to sink through our perpetual brain fog. We memorize the important verses of scripture, or at least, we hear them over and over again until they are tattooed in our minds, but they still hover just below the surface of our skin. Once in a while, if we are truly blessed, the fog lifts and the message makes our vital signs spring to life. We become more completely who we were meant to be by loving God more completely. It is as simple and as frightening as that.

■ ■ ■

Day by day, O dear Lord, three things I pray - To see thee more clearly, love thee more dearly, follow thee more nearly, day by day. Amen.

November 3

Jeremiah 31:33-34
But this covenant that I will make with the house of Israel
after those days, says the Lord: I will put my law within
them, and I will write it on their hearts; and I will be their
God, and they shall be my people. No longer shall they
teach one another, or say to each other, "Know the Lord,"
for they shall all know me, from the least of them to the
greatest, says the Lord; for I will forgive their iniquity, and
remember their sin no more.

■ ■ ■

Our desire to know the Lord could rarely be described as a
quest. A quest implies a focused commitment. A desire is a
fleeting thing that comes and goes. We have to be reminded
sometimes that knowing God is something worthwhile. We
will pursue it if we are convinced that there is something
"in it for us." And so, throughout the history of the people of
God, we have been sent prophets to remind us to "know the
Lord." It seems ironic to me that while we are busy trying
to remember God. God is busy forgetting our sins -
including our forgetfulness. The part of God which is the
most knowable is his willingness to forgive us for forgetting
him. When we love someone, we don't want them to have to
work so hard at loving us.

■ ■ ■

Lord, forgive us and please don't give up on us. Amen.

November 4

Psalm 46:10
Be still, and know that I am God!

■ ■ ■

If only we had stoplights in the other places of our lives besides on streets. Imagine a stoplight in the kitchen or the living room or the garage. Something to stop us - not permanently - but momentarily so that our thoughts and emotions have a chance to catch up with the rest of us like a small child chasing a long-legged mother. A stoplight before we reacted in anger might give us just enough time to cool off. A stoplight in the ever increasing burdens of daily schedules might remind us of a bigger picture, a greater hope. A stoplight might help us remember just who we are and who God is and help us to enjoy....even if only for a moment...all that is truly right and good in the world.

■ ■ ■

Lord God, gently bring us to a still moment in which we might know your purpose and our place, know your grace and the enormity of love. Amen.

November 5

Romans 3:19
Now we know that whatever the law says, it speaks to those who are under the law, so that every mouth may be silenced, and the whole world may be held accountable to God.

■ ■ ■

In the former sitcom "Grace under Fire," the lead character speculated about God in one episode and imagined that God must get rather tired of our constant prayers that sound more like a childish "Gimmee" list. Grace said, "Somewhere, up there....God is shaking his head and going - 'Blah, Blah, Blah.' Since I can imagine a God of infinite patience and since God is greater than my imagination, then I doubt he "yada, yada, yada's" our prayers. But God does have a way of silencing us for our own good. He does it with his grace. Like a magnificent sunset, a mountain vista, a rolling ocean, a sea of winter wheat, the mystery of a child.....where we just stand in awe and silence to take it in...when we truly behold the grace of God, we are silenced to our knees.

■ ■ ■

Lord God, help us not to take for granted the cost of your love and the enormity of your grace. Amen.

November 6

John 8:31-32
Jesus said to the Jews who had believed in him, "If you continue in my word, you are truly my disciples; and you will know the truth, and the truth will make you free.

■ ■ ■

There are lots of great sayings about the truth. "The truth hurts." or "The truth will make us free but first it will make us miserable." or that great Jack Nicholson movie line "You want the truth? You can't handle the truth!" There is a great freedom in knowing and accepting the truth, but often that only happens after slicing through the entwined tissue of our elaborate denial and wishful thinking. The truth is skin peeled back, exposed and vulnerable. The necrotic tissue is cut away. The infection of lies is removed. Miraculously, we survive the necessary surgery and we are alive to face another day wounded, but alive. We can bury ourselves inside the lies of our own making or experience the freedom which abounds in the truth of our sin and God's grace.

■ ■ ■

Lord, help us to accept the truth and embrace the freedom of forgiveness. Amen.

November 7

Revelation 7:16-17
They will hunger no more, and thirst no more; the sun will not strike them, nor any scorching heat; for the Lamb at the center of the throne will be their shepherd, and he will guide them to springs of the water of life, and God will wipe away every tear from their eyes.

■ ■ ■

Every 5 seconds a person dies of hunger-related causes. Millions of people have no access to safe drinking water. We have all the resources we need to end hunger and provide access to clean water for the whole world. The issues related to why we aren't doing it are complicated by political power, economics and squeakier wheels getting more attention. In the Revelation, picture John paints of paradise, at the top of God's list is taking care of the hungry and the thirsty. On those days when we are struggling to know God's will, perhaps we could put aside our own to-do lists and take a look at God's.

■ ■ ■

Give us a passion for justice, Lord, so that all may be full and whole in you. Amen.

November 8

Amos 5:14-15
Seek good and not evil, that you may live; and so the Lord,
the God of hosts, will be with you, just as you have said.
Hate evil and love good, and establish justice in the gate; it
may be that the Lord, the God of hosts, will be gracious to
the remnant of Joseph.

■ ■ ■

I read a letter to the editor in our town newspaper the other day written by a woman thanking a man for a random act of kindness. He had noticed she had difficulty with opening a coin-operated box to purchase a morning paper so he slipped his own coins in the slot and bought one for her. It was such a surprising and selfless gesture she was motivated to express her own appreciation publically. It made me ache that such tiny acts of kindness to a stranger would be news worthy. We learn to be gracious when we have known grace. The people of God have no excuse for not being gracious, gentle, forbearing of others. We make our way - day by day and step by step - by being reminded of the basics. Seek good and not evil. God will not let go of his people.

■ ■ ■

Lord God, help us to recognize evil and good when we see it and to seek your gracious face in all our days so that your grace may be seen in us. Amen.

November 9

Psalm 90:12
So teach us to number our days, that we may apply our
hearts to wisdom.

■ ■ ■

"How do you measure a life?" The question is asked in a
song from the musical "Rent." Do we measure it in sunsets,
in midnights, in cups of coffee, in laughter, or in strife?
When I have gathered with families before a funeral, I have
listened to their stories - their summary of a life lived. It is
measured not in minutes or years, but in meals, moments,
personality, and passions. We can measure our life with
sorrow or joy, hardships or celebrations, or we can measure
the days of our lives with the love we have known through
the cross of Jesus Christ.

■ ■ ■

Holy God, be gracious to your servants and remind us of
your ceaseless love. Amen.

November 10

Hebrews 4:12-13
Indeed, the word of God is living and active, sharper than
any two-edged sword, piercing until it divides soul from
spirit, joints from Marrow; it is able to judge the thoughts
and intentions of the heart. And before him no creature is
hidden, but all are naked and laid bare to the eyes of the
one to whom we must render an account.

■ ■ ■

Thanks to some high-tech tools, there are some surgeries that can be performed that are classified as "non-invasive." A person's body doesn't have to be cut wide open in order for the procedure to be done. There are times, however, where the situation calls for a more invasive process. The miracle of God's surgical skill is that he is able to see what is hidden and expose what is wrong and still promise us life. To let him work his way in our lives we must accept that something needs healing and trust that God can do surgery from the inside out.

■ ■ ■

Master Designer and Holy Physician, hold us gently in your gracious hands and heal us. Amen.

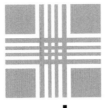

November 11

Isaiah 53:4-5

Surely he has borne our infirmities and carried our diseases; yet we accounted him stricken, struck down by God, and afflicted. But he was wounded for our transgressions, crushed for our iniquities; upon him was the punishment that made us whole, and by his bruises we are healed.

■ ■ ■

I know a person who, when he was a college student, had a large cross tattooed on his back. It means a great deal to him. It was an affirmation of his faith during a journey which had been filled with some rough patches. The difficult times did not magically go away after this affirmation of faith. While talking with him one day when he seemed to be carrying the weight of the world on his shoulders, I asked him to consider leaning against the cross that had come to mean so much to him. His journey of faith might marked by how he bore his cross but also how he leaned into it. We often forget that the burdens we bear and the sins we commit are the stuff that Jesus died on the cross to redeem. He has born our grief and our punishment. Though we still have wounds, we can be freed from our guilt and given the strength and the hope to live.

■ ■ ■

Holy God, when what we bear is too heavy, help us to take it to the cross and leave it there. Amen.

November 12

Psalm 91:1,4
You who live in the shelter of the Most High, who abide in
the shadow of the Almighty; he will cover you with his
pinions, and under his wings you will find refuge; his
faithfulness is a shield and buckler.

■ ■ ■

As the psalmist sings a song for us of the character of God,
he strikes a chord that vibrates deeply in our psyches - the
need for safety - a place in which we are protected from
harm. Such a place had often been imagined as a literal
place - a fortress, a castle, a walled city. But the image here
is of a mother bird gathering chicks beneath the shelter of
her wings. The sheltering bird becomes the fortress for her
children. That is the simple image that defines our
relationship with God. In order to know the depth and
power of that relationship we must become who we are -
little children hiding beneath God's wing at God's
invitation.

■ ■ ■

Holy God, humble us to the size of children and beckon us
run to your wings. Amen.

317

November 13

John 4: 23
The true worshipers will worship the Father in spirit and truth

■ ■ ■

One of the great occupational hazards for pastors is that sometimes we forget to worship. Responsible for the mechanics of the worship celebration, we think more about what comes next than focusing on God. The danger of not paying attention to the task is stumbling or missing words. The last thing I want to do is have my mistake become the focus of attention, so there is some justifiable defense of attending to the business of worship. I have learned that, out in the pews, it is just as challenging to keep focused on the worship. Children squirm, someone is remembering the argument with a family member in the parking lot or wondering what's for lunch. Even still, on the chords of a hymn, in the flicker of a candle, in the aroma of the bread, in the exquisite warmth of a human hand, in words almost too wonderful to understand completely, we worship together. Even still, the truth and the Spirit surround the people and in our feeble, distracted way we praise God.

■ ■ ■

Lord God, receive the work of our worship as a gift to you who loves us so well. Amen.

November 14

Jeremiah 31:33-34
But this is the covenant that I will make with the house of
Israel after those days, says the Lord: I will put my law
within them, and I will write it on their hearts; and I will
be their God, and they shall be my people. No longer shall
they teach one another, or say to each other, "Know the
Lord," for they shall all know me, from the least of them to
the greatest, says the Lord; for I will forgive their iniquity,
and remember their sin no more.

■ ■ ■

In sign language, the sign for 'learn' involves cupping one
hand upward and gesturing with the other in a way that
looks like you are lifting something out of the cupped hand
and physically putting that thing into your head. For
centuries the covenant between God and God's people had
that kind of character. Knowledge being placed from the
outside in. The new covenant God has promised is one that
moves from the inside out. Sin is forgiven. All will know
God. Who we are in baptism and at the Lord's table is a
glimpse of that promise fulfilled. We cannot yet abandon
the work of putting the knowledge of God into our heads
but we can also trust that God is working on our hearts
from the inside out.

■ ■ ■

Write your law upon our hearts, Lord. Amen.

November 15

Psalm 46:11
Be still, then, and know that I am God; I will be exalted
among the nations; I will be exalted in the earth. The Lord
of hosts is with us; the God of Jacob is our stronghold.

■ ■ ■

We don't do "still" well. Being still happens when we fall exhausted into bed, but the rest of the time we are moving, multi-tasking, thinking, worrying, planning, plotting. Sometimes we need someone to tell us to "hush" - to listen even if it starts with hearing our own breathing, the pulse of our heart, or the ringing in our ears from the last noise that vibrated our eardrums. We hear our own old thoughts thundering around inside our head until they, too, weary of themselves and they sit like a sullen teenager slumping in an overstuffed chair. And then, perhaps, we finally hear something besides our own voice. We hear God.

■ ■ ■

In the stillness, speak to us, Lord. Amen.

November 16

Romans 3:19-20
Now we know that whatever the law says, it speaks to those who are under the law, so that every mouth may be silenced, and the whole world may be held accountable to God. For "no human being will be justified in his sight" by deeds prescribed by the law, for through the law comes the knowledge of sin.

■ ■ ■

We all fall short. It is so easy to say, "No one's perfect!" There is a blissful balm in keeping the confession in broad-brush, general terms. It is when we are faced with a very specific sin, an error in judgment, a thoughtless or selfish moment that we squirm. When that sin has caused the grief of others, it compounds the weight and the hopelessness of it all. Some of the sweetest words of our worship liturgy reflect the scriptures, "To whom shall we go? You have the words of eternal life." God does hold us accountable. The good news is that God holds us.

■ ■ ■

We stand before you, Lord, guilty of what we have done and left undone. Forgive us. Amen.

November 17

John 1: 38
When Jesus turned and saw them following, he said to them, "What are you looking for?"

■ ■ ■

The beginning portions of the Gospel of John are simple statements and questions. "What are you looking for?" We take no journey unless we know why we are going. When we look to Jesus and consider following, it is in response to a deep need in our lives that we may not have even dared to articulate. We may not yet know what we need or want. A Danish poet named Piet Hein once wrote that if you are having trouble making a decision between some options - toss a coin - not that the decision will be made on a coin flip but if left to chance, at the moment the coin is in the air you would know what you are hoping. It is that hope that might inform our decisions. Our relationship with Jesus is sown in the soil of our hope for relief from the brokenness of our own making and for wholeness beyond our ability to create. We hope in Christ and look to him.

■ ■ ■

Holy God, be patient with us as we sort through the confusion and begin to see more clearly. Amen.

322

November 18

I Thessalonians 2:5-8
As you know and as God is our witness, we never came with
words of flattery or with a pretext for greed; nor did we seek
praise from mortals, whether from you or from others,
though we might have made demands as apostles of Christ.
But we were gentle among you, like a nurse tenderly caring
for her own children. So deeply do we care for you that we
are determined to share with you not only the gospel of God
but also our own selves, because you have become very dear
to us.

■　■　■

The Apostle Paul is one who understands the power and the
limitation of words. I often forget how easily words can be
rebuffed and treated as empty shells with no substance. As
powerful as the internet has become as a tool for the
transmission of words to one another, it is still not a
substitute for presence, an understanding look, a heartfelt
gesture, an extended hand. We are, like Paul, to be "gentle
among you." To those we hold dear we offer the best of who
we are - the gospel of God pulled through us and everything
we are along with it.

■　■　■

Precious Lord, you showed your love for us by being wholly
present and gently among us even at the cost of your life.
May we be more like you. Amen.

November 19

I John 3:2-3
Beloved, we are God's children now; what we will be has not
yet been revealed. What we do know is this: when he is
revealed, we will be like him, for we will see him as he is.
And all who have this hope in him purify themselves, just
as he is pure.

■ ■ ■

Oh, the irony. At my elbow as I write this is an envelope
which contains a draft of my will and medical power of
attorney. There are lots of words scattered throughout like
death, terminal, irreversible condition, life support, pain
medication. This is painful to read. I am not sick, but I
haven't even seen the attorney's bill yet! I shoved it aside
and turned to the scriptures for today. Whatever happens,
it says, you and I are children of God now and we will be
like God when all is said and done. Works for me. Where do
I sign?

■ ■ ■

Holy God, thank you for making us permanent members of
your family so that we have nothing to fear. Amen.

November 20

Zephaniah 1:18
Neither their silver nor their gold will be able to save them on the day of the Lord's wrath; in the fire of his passion the whole earth shall be consumed; for a full, a terrible end he will make of all the inhabitants of the earth.

■ ■ ■

In the musical "Mame", the lead character finds herself in need of some good news for a change and she sings "For I've grown a little leaner, grown a little colder, grown a little sadder, grown a little older, and I need a little angel sitting on my shoulder, need a little Christmas now." The news of the prophet speaks of God's anger on account of our sin, selfishness, greed, and disobedience. Nothing we have will be able to buy our way back into God's favor. God has the power to raze the world and start over again as he wills. The headlines from our newspaper don't give us much hope either. We need some good news. We need a little Christmas. Right this very minute. We need an Easter too. So Merry Christmas - Christ is born! Happy Easter - Christ is Risen! Now let's start to live today like people who have heard and believe the Good News.

■ ■ ■

Lord God, fill us with your good news so that we might be your holy people alive today because you came to be among us, died for us and rose again. Amen.

325

November 21

Psalm 90:4
For a thousand years in your sight are like yesterday when
it is past, or like a watch in the night

■ ■ ■

Where does the day go? Where did the week disappear to? Time flows through the fingers of our lives at a dizzy pace. We can account for the time - we need to sleep, eat, travel to work and school, maintain the household, and study. That consumes the hours of the day. That is accounting for our time. I count the 56 minutes I spent with a friend today like no other cluster of minutes in my day. It is 56 minutes of splashing my feet on the edge of the Kingdom of God. It is holy time because God is so eternally present when we gather. No matter the topic of conversation - the time is made holy and as valuable as a night's sleep or a whole Saturday at play. A child of God punches a different type of time clock.

■ ■ ■

Teach us, O Lord, to measure our days with our hearts turned toward you. Amen.

November 22

I Thessalonians 5: 8,11
But since we belong to the day, let us be sober, and put on the breastplate of faith and love, and for a helmet the hope of salvation. Therefore encourage one another and build up each other, as indeed you are doing.

■ ■ ■

Two of the deep, underlying purposes of boot camp for military training are for soldiers to learn obedience to orders and loyalty to the soldiers fighting alongside them. No one wants to send troops into battle who cannot be trusted to follow orders. When soldiers watch out for each other, it breeds a sense of strength and courage that is born of loyalty even when patriotism waxes and wanes. In the daily trenches of life, our defense against cruelty is faith, love and hope in God. An even better defense is to use our faith, love, and hope to lift one another up and trust that Christ of the trenches is doing the same for us.

■ ■ ■

Lord, march with us in the battle against human cruelty and thoughtlessness and give us the confidence of your victory. Amen.

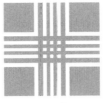

November 23

Matthew 25:23-25
His master said to him, 'Well done, good and trustworthy
slave; you have been trustworthy in a few things, I will put
you in charge of many things; enter into the joy of your
master.' Then the one who had received the one talent also
came forward, saying, 'Master, I knew you were a harsh
man, reaping where you did not sow, and gathering where
you did not scatter seed; so I was afraid, and I went and hid
your talent in the ground. Here you have what is yours.'

■ ■ ■

I talked with a group of students about how to measure
Christian maturity for the purpose of knowing if and in
what way we may need to grow. Certainly prayer, Bible
reading, worship, service to others are areas of growth in
discipleship. Our relationship with God and with one
another is an important aspect of following Jesus as well.
Christian maturity in our relationships does not mean we
are perfect, but it means that we foster an environment of
trust. Are we trustworthy? Do we trust others? When trust
is broken, do we trust the process of confession and
forgiveness to heal and restore our relationships? Are we
good stewards of God's confidence in us?

■ ■ ■

Lord God, may we grow up in every way so that everyone
might experience the joy of your salvation. Amen.

November 24

Ezekiel 34:11-12
Thus says the Lord God: I myself will search for my sheep,
and will seek them out. As shepherds seek out their flocks
when they are among their scattered sheep, so I will seek
out my sheep. I will rescue them from all the places to
which they have been scattered on a day of clouds and thick
darkness.

■　■　■

I have a variety of little sheep figures in my office. I have collected them or received them as gifts. They are reminders of my call to tend God's flock. One of my favorites is a wood carving of a sheep scratching its ear with its hind foot. Scratching an ear is a gesture we make when we are confused, trying to think, or feeling totally clueless. The confused-looking sheep is a reminder to me of the daily moments when I am confused and not even aware that I have gone astray. And it reminds me of the people I am called to serve who are often in the same condition. In the midst of this is our beloved Shepherd with sleeves rolled up, relentless in his mission and headed in our direction.

■　■　■

Holy God, gather your scattered little ones and guide us with your wisdom and mercy. Amen.

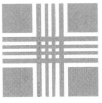

November 25

Psalm 95:76-8a
For he is our God, and we are the people of his pasture, and the sheep of his hand. O that today you would listen to his voice! Do not harden your hearts

■ ■ ■

There is a Robert Frost poem that says, "The sun was warm but the wind was chill. You know how it is with an April day When the sun is out and the wind is still, You're one month on in the middle of May. But if you so much as dare to speak, A cloud comes over the sunlit arch, A wind comes off a frozen peak, And you're two months back in the middle of March." Just as quickly as a turn in the weather, we harden our hearts toward God and toward one another. The warm image of the shepherd caring for his sheep is lost behind the cold shield. Our instinct for our own survival and protection from hurt kicks in and overrides our trust in the one who has promised so much. But our instinct to hide only leaves us cold. The Lord shines and offers warmth even and especially in a cold front if we dare to keep our hearts open.

■ ■ ■

Protect us, O Lord, from our own tendency to protect ourselves. Make us willing to be vulnerable to your will and open to your loving Spirit. Amen.

November 26

Ephesians 1:16-18a
I pray that the God of our Lord Jesus Christ, the Father of
glory, may give you a spirit of wisdom and revelation as you
come to know him, so that, with the eyes of your heart
enlightened, you may know what is the hope to which he
has called you

■ ■ ■

Getting our head and heart working together has been one of the great challenges of being human. Our head needs to be fed with knowledge, but information alone doesn't make us wise. Wisdom flows - it moves from the inside out because we want to share what we have seen and heard. Wisdom flows from the heart - its vehicle is love. I can't imagine anything better that I could pray for those for whom I care than to desire that their heads and hearts are working together. I pray that they are growing in the knowledge of God and that their way is guided by the eyes of their hearts.

■ ■ ■

May we, Lord, this day be known by our faith in Christ and by our love for your people. Amen.

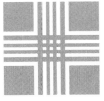

November 27

Matthew 25:37,40
Then the righteous will answer him, "Lord, when was it
that we saw you hungry and gave you food, or thirsty and
gave you something to drink? And the king will answer
them, "Truly I tell you, just as you did it to one of the least
of these who are members of my family, you did it to me."

■　■　■

We speak of a person being the "pillar" of the church or the community. The righteous are such pillars. God chooses to use them to hold up the world and the amazing thing is that they don't even know who they are. The ones who love without limits, without regard to anything else about a person but their need, are the ones who God calls righteous. Through the cross of Christ we are declared righteous ˙ made right with God and therefore free to love without limits. We can be the house where the empty are held and fed. One person at a time, through the power of the cross, we can hold up the world.

■　■　■

Holy God, make me an instrument of your peace and make my heart a home for those in need. Amen.

November 28

Isaiah 64:8-9
Yet, O LORD, you are our Father; we are the clay, and you are our potter; we are all the work of your hand. Do not be exceedingly angry, O LORD, and do not remember iniquity forever. Now consider, we are all your people.

■ ■ ■

I talked to a mother recently who said of her daughter, "I know she came out of me but there are days when I don't know where she came from!" I can imagine that the Lord has those days too. Throughout the scriptures, prophets, patriarchs, and poets have appealed to God for mercy and leniency despite humanity's bad behavior. The one pathetic cry they all have in common is "Lord, we are your creation; please don't give up on us." Whether the cry actually works or not, we don't truly know. All that we know for certain is that God never has given up on his creation. For some, that is license to run recklessly through their lives. For others, it means beginning every day saying "Given everything you have done for me, Lord, what can I do for you today?"

■ ■ ■

Take my life, Lord, that it may be a source of joy and pride to you. Amen.

November 29

I Corinthians 1:4-6
I give thanks to my God always for you because of the grace
of God that has been given you in Christ Jesus, for in every
way you have been enriched in him, in speech and
knowledge of every kind- just as the testimony of Christ has
been strengthened among you

■ ■ ■

One of the gifts that we receive from those whose opinion
and perspective we value is the opportunity to see ourselves
in their eyes. I have not always liked what I have been
shown. I have seen my weaknesses, inconsistencies, and
self-pity. The miracle of grace is being given the knowledge
of sin, but the freedom from condemnation so that we might
find the right path again. Paul walked with the Corinthians
through their foolishness and inconsistency and lifted them
up to one who could restore them to life. Another gift not to
be underestimated is the power of the most encouraging
word so that perhaps someone might see Jesus in us.

■ ■ ■

Thank you, Lord, for those who reveal your grace to us
through their gentle honesty and their constant
encouragement. Amen.

November 30

Isaiah 40:10-11
*See, the Lord God comes with might, and his arm rules for
him; his reward is with him, and his recompense before
him. He will gather the lambs in his arms, and carry them
in his bosom, and gently lead the mother sheep.*

■ ■ ■

While hiking in New Zealand, I bunked with a couple of
women from Australia - a mother and daughter. The
daughter was a mother herself and had some rough times
with relationships and jobs. Though not a person of any
particular faith, she freely confessed that she survived all
the difficult times because she said, "I have me mum." Her
"mum" is a great woman who loves her children with
vitality and passion. There were times, however, when even
the greatest of comforters need comforting. The wonderful
news of the Advent season is that the Lord is coming - He is
coming to gather and comfort - He is coming even to comfort
the comforters.

■ ■ ■

Come, Lord Jesus, with your comforting arms, your
compassionate heart, and your mission to save. Amen.

December 1

Psalm 85:8
Let me hear what God the LORD will speak, for he will speak peace to his people, to his faithful, to those who turn to him in their hearts.

■ ■ ■

The comedian, Bill Crosby, in a standup routine explained how he would call to his toddler son. He would say in a calm voice, "Come 'ere" and then after no response, repeat and repeat "Come 'ere, come 'ere, come 'ere, come 'ere!" We sometimes bemoan that God does not seem to be speaking today. He has had plenty to say to people from ancient days, but doesn't seem to have spoken in a more contemporary setting. The scriptures contain all that we need to hear and know about grace, hope, our future and the nature of the God who loves us. He said, "Come 'ere" once and gave us the scriptures so that we could hear it over and over and over again - until the message starts to find our hearts.

■ ■ ■

Help us to hear your word today in the ancient words of the scriptures made anew everyday in your love and grace for us. Amen.

December 2

2 Peter 3:10-11
But the day of the Lord will come like a thief, and then the heavens will pass away with a loud noise, and the elements will be dissolved with fire, and the earth and everything that is done on it will be disclosed. Since all these things are to be dissolved in this way, what sort of persons ought you to be in leading lives of holiness and godliness?

■ ■ ■

There is something chilling about this verse. There is a sense that when the day of the Lord comes we will be caught naked with all our flaws showing. Exposed will be everything we have done and left undone. All of the hearts we have broken, lives we have disappointed, hurt we have caused, loneliness we have ignored, and injustice we have left to fester. What if we were faced with all that we tuck away in the crevices of our human clutter hoping for some magical yard sale at which someone else will make the messes we have created disappear. The day of the Lord is coming. We will stand utterly vulnerable before the Lord. I expect that moment to be colossally uncomfortable. But given who God is and what he has done for you and me, I can't imagine wanting to be anywhere else on the day of the Lord. The discomfort will dissolve quickly into joy for the children of God.

■ ■ ■

O come, O come, Emmanuel and ransom captive Israel....and while you are at it, Lord, save me. Amen.

337

December 3

Isaiah 25:6-7
On this mountain the Lord of hosts will make for all peoples
a feast of rich food, a feast of well-aged wines, of rich food
filled with marrow, of well-aged wines strained clear. And
he will destroy on this mountain the shroud that is cast
over all the peoples, the sheet that is spread over all
nations; he will swallow up death forever.

■ ■ ■

Part of the experience of Holy Communion is that we are
given a glimpse of the Kingdom of God. Through the bread
and the wine, the wall between this kingdom and the next
grows thin and almost translucent like a window. We can
press our noses against the window and peek into heaven.
We get a foretaste of the feast to come. Strangely enough it
is like looking at a mirror. What we can see for certain is
that we are there and Christ is there with us. The only
difference is that we can only get a peek, a taste of what
will be a way of life in God's Kingdom. What we know for
certain about heaven is that Christ is there and there is a
place for us at the victory celebration.

■ ■ ■

Come, Lord Jesus. Amen.

December 4

Revelations 21:5-6

And the one who was seated on the throne said, "See, I am making all things new." Also he said, "Write this, for these words are trustworthy and true." Then he said to me, "It is done! I am the Alpha and the Omega, the beginning and the end. To the thirsty I will give water as a gift from the spring of the water of life.

■ ■ ■

When the volcano Mount St. Helen erupted, it blew the top off the mountain. The explosion destroyed forests, homes, and lives and turned a crystalline-clear, mountain lake into a muddy stew with thousands of trees that had been ripped from their roots. The scene of destruction was massive and changed the landscape forever. It wasn't long, however, before the first sprouts of living plant life pushed their way through the broken forest and ash to find the sun. God makes all things new and wanted us to believe it too. It starts again with the water of life.

■ ■ ■

Holy God, we come to the spring to be made clean, to drink, and to be made new. Amen.

December 5

I Kings 17:14-16
For thus says the Lord the God of Israel: The jar of meal
will not be emptied and the jug of oil will not fail until the
day that the Lord sends rain on the earth." She went and
did as Elijah said, so that she as well as he and her
household ate for many days. The jar of meal was not
emptied, neither did the jug of oil fail, according to the word
of the Lord that he spoke by Elijah.

■ ■ ■

The Lord commanded a widow with little food to keep
herself and her son alive to sustain his prophet Elijah
during a famine. No matter who he was, Elijah was to her
just another mouth to feed. She showed Elijah the
desperate nature of the situation and Elijah offered her the
promise of the Lord's provision. The Lord does provide. But
the provision came to them not in a storehouse of supplies
that would be good for months. Provision came in the
promise of God each day that the jar of meal and oil would
not fail. Trust in God is something that must happen on a
daily basis. Sometimes it happens from meal to meal.

■ ■ ■

Holy God, we trust you from one meal to the next and
thank you for your provision. Amen.

December 6

Exodus 18:22
Let them sit as judges for the people at all times; let them
bring every important case to you, but decide every minor
case themselves. So it will be easier for you, and they will
bear the burden with you.

■ ■ ■

Moses was having a customer service problem. The line of people waiting for him to hear their civil disputes was wrapped around the building. Moses' father-in-law must have been the first management consultant in recorded history. His solution was simple: Delegate authority. He appointed and trained judges to handle the smaller claims. The risk in delegating authority is that the task may not be done exactly the way we would have done it. Perhaps a decision is made that we might not have made. For the people of Israel, the community life was mired in the process of solving disputes that could have been settled quickly. The risk of losing some control versus the value of time and peace must be weighed carefully. Moses chose to trust others with God's justice for the sake of the people and himself. God's justice is a task that has been delegated to us with his help and guidance.

■ ■ ■

Lord God, teach us to share our responsibilities and walk with you every day. Amen.

December 7

Hebrews 9:26b-28
But as it is, he has appeared once for all at the end of the
age to remove sin by the sacrifice of himself. And just as it
is appointed for mortals to die once, and after that the
judgment, so Christ, having been offered once to bear the
sins of many will appear a second time, not to deal with sin,
but to save those who are eagerly waiting for him.

■ ■ ■

The tiny crosses that we wear around our necks may lull us
into forgetting how big the cross of Christ is. The death of
God's Son for the sake of the world looms large and casts
not a shadow but a light. It takes on all of our darkness. It
is big enough to bear our sins. To believe that our sin is too
great for God's forgiveness to is an insult to the magnitude
of Christ's sacrifice. To underestimate the power of the
cross is to languish in the darkness.

■ ■ ■

Holy God, we expose our darkness to your light and await
your coming again. Amen.

December 8

Mark 12:43-44
Then he called his disciples and said to them, "Truly I tell you, this poor widow has put in more than all those who are contributing to the treasury. For all of them have contributed out of their abundance; but she out of her poverty has put in everything she had, all she had to live on."

■ ■ ■

The more I learn about trusting in God's care and provision, the more I learn how much I have to learn. Just when I think I am paddling away just fine in the deep end of the pool, the pool turns into an ocean and the perils unknown grow vast. Jesus gave his disciples a way to look at the world and other people. Jesus helped us all to see that God is not only watching but is intimately affected by those who trust him the most. The ocean is very big and we are very small, but God never loses sight of us.

■ ■ ■

Holy God, help us to trust you completely. Amen.

December 9

Daniel 12:1,3
At that time Michael, the great prince, the protector of your
people, shall arise. There shall be a time of anguish, such as
has never occurred since nations first came into existence.
But at that time your people shall be delivered, everyone
who is found written in the book. Those who are wise shall
shine like the brightness of the sky, and those who lead
many to righteousness, like the stars forever and ever.

■ ■ ■

To a people feeling downtrodden and hopeless, the Old
Testament prophets were charged by God to give them a
vision of a new world. It was a vision that would lift them
up and help them remain faithful to God. Their picture
wasn't "pie in the sky" by any means. It was always laced
with the promise that God had made with them and would
not break. Wisdom according to the scriptures begins with
the fear of the Lord. That is the kind of wisdom that shines
in the face of the darkest facts.

■ ■ ■

On our knees, O Lord, we come. We are aware of your
power and ask for your mercy. Amen.

December 10

2 Samuel 7:12-13
When your days are fulfilled and you lie down with your ancestors, I will raise up your offspring after you, who shall come forth from your body, and I will establish his kingdom. He shall build a house for my name, and I will establish the throne of his kingdom forever.

■ ■ ■

King David decided that the ark of the covenant needed a proper house not just a tent. God reminded King David of his shepherd boy days. God had made him a king and that God would decide the details about his own house and who would build it. No matter whether we own or rent, it is good to be reminded that we are all still tenants. I saw a man yesterday working very hard at putting lights on the outside of his house - lights more neighbors and strangers would ever see and appreciate than him or his family. I doubt he was climbing a ladder on a cold day for the likes of strangers. He was doing it for his own pride and his own family. Even for the fleeting moments as he drove in the driveway, the house would look as he would want it to look. God's chastising words to David were filled with love and promise. God will establish his kingdom as he wills....the amazing thing is that God climbs the ladder and strings the lights for us.

■ ■ ■

Shine, Jesus, shine that we may know your truth and follow your light. Amen.

December 11

Hebrews 10:24-25
And let us consider how to provoke one another to love and good deeds, not neglecting to meet together, as is the habit of some, but encouraging one another, and all the more as you see the Day approaching.

■ ■ ■

I have learned much about the advantages and disadvantages of email as a vehicle for communication. Its speed and ease of use is light years ahead of pens and stationary and postage. There is, however, much to be misunderstood when words are conveyed so thoughtlessly without the sound of a human voice, the sight of a tear, the flash of an angry eye, or the touch of a compassionate hand. The tools of communication still pale in comparison to the power of one another's presence. God sent messengers but none had such a profound effect on the world as when God came himself as a human being among us. Without even saying many words, our presence can provoke others to love and good deeds.

■ ■ ■

We gather together to ask the Lord's blessing. He hastens and chastens his will to make known. Thanks be to God. Amen.

346

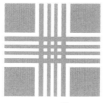

December 12

Daniel 7:13-14
As I watched in the night visions, I saw one like a human being coming with the clouds of heaven. And he came to the Ancient One and presented before him. To him was given dominion and glory and kingship, that all peoples, nations, and languages should serve him. His dominion is an everlasting dominion that shall not pass away, and his kingship is one that shall never be destroyed.

■ ■ ■

In the midst of a vision filled with magnificent heavenly images is one human being. We expect great things. We expect that the one who shall come will be bigger than life, possessing all the gifts necessary, someone who is all things to all people. The people of Israel wanted not just a leader but a king. Someone bigger than life. Someone greater than themselves. God sent us a human being. In doing so, God raises all of humanity to a height that puts us within arm's reach of him. In sending us a human being - His Son, our humanness took on a dignity that we often underestimate. Jesus led not by being in the possession of a remarkable skill set. Jesus led by being authentically human.

■ ■ ■

Holy God, help us not to be repulsed by our humanity but accepting of who we are and how you made us. Amen.

December 13

Psalm 93:1-2
The Lord is king, he is robed in majesty; the Lord is robed,
he is girded with strength. He has established the world; it
shall never be moved

■ ■ ■

At church camp, it wasn't unusual to have at least one homesick youth and a few bored ones. As long as they were doing something, they were laughing and content. As soon as there was any down time at all, they complained of boredom and longed for home. I took a group of them out to stand beneath a tree. I had them look up through the shining green ceiling of its leaves, the blue sky rolling with wisps of clouds. It was a stained glass window unique in all the world. It existed only the moment and just for them like the sounds of a symphony. I taught them again how to say "Wow!" to God. I tried to erase the word 'bored' from their vocabulary. The Lord our God is with us. The Lord our God is amazing. The Lord our God and the world he established is worthy of our constant "Wow!"

■ ■ ■

Mighty Lord, we give you praise for this most amazing day! Amen.

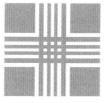

December 14

Jeremiah 33:14-15
The days are surely coming, says the Lord, when I will
fulfill the promise I made to the house of Israel and the
house of Judah. In those days and at that time I will cause
a righteous Branch to spring up for David; and he shall
execute justice and righteousness in the land.

■ ■ ■

We are all better at recognizing injustice than we are at
doing anything to change that injustice. I have a friend who
when his children complain with the words, "That's not
fair!" his response to his children is, "Well, we are NOT the
Fair Family!" Children have not yet learned that absolute
fairness - though sounding good in principle - is a slippery
slope. We want fairness, but there are more times when we
need the second chance, the do-over, or the act of grace. We
have a hair trigger at recognizing unfairness, but are less
quick and less powerful to address it. The Lord our God
fulfills, causes, executes justice and righteousness.
Sometimes the first step toward justice is simply trusting in
the one who is less concerned about fairness and more
concerned that we are in his family.

■ ■ ■

Holy God, stir in us the ability to trust in your promises.
Amen.

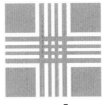

December 15

Psalm 25:2-3

My God, I put my trust in you; let me not be put to shame, nor let my enemies triumph over me. Let none who look to you be put to shame; rather let those be put to shame who are treacherous.

■ ■ ■

The ancient people of Israel were often in a position of powerlessness. They were at the mercy of enemies from without and within. When their enemies triumphed and did the victory dance, the loss was even more bitter. Our enemies take different forms today but still we fight the dragons. I saw a drawing of a dragon which was finishing a snack on what was left of the knight who came to slay it. The dragon was picking its teeth with the knight's lance. the caption read, "Sometimes the dragon wins." We know from experience there is truth in it. To whom shall we go? What then shall we do? The scriptures echo our realistic grasp of the nature of our plight. As Corrie ten Boom once wrote from her own experience with suffering – "there is no pit so dark or deep where Christ is not deeper still." Trusting, even in the face of snacking dragons, is a day to day, sometimes even hour to hour battle against the darkness.

■ ■ ■

O Lord, hear my prayer, surround me with the power of your salvation. Amen.

December 16

I Thessalonians 3:9-10
How can we thank God enough for you in return for all the
joy that we feel before our God because of you? Night and
day we pray most earnestly that we may see you face to
face and restore whatever is lacking in your faith.

■ ■ ■

Our faith, our ability to believe in the miraculous grace of
God and the wildly illogical resurrection of Jesus Christ on
our behalf, is itself - a gift. God grants us the ability to
believe. That faith, however, needs attention. It needs
nourishment to grow and thrive. It becomes anemic when
we don't feed it regularly and well. Beyond the lip of the cup
of coffee, the marks on the table from children's craft
projects, beyond the plate of cinnamon toast and eggs, are
faces and eyes that may provide some of the food that we
need for this day of the Gospel journey. In the company of
one another we have the opportunity to restore one
another's faith and create joy. We are given the ability to
deliver love.

■ ■ ■

Thank you, God, for the faith to believe in your love and the
faith to give it away. Amen.

December 17

Luke 21:25-26
Be on guard so that your hearts are not weighed down with
dissipation and drunkenness and the worries of this life,
and that day catch you unexpectedly, like a trap. For it will
come upon all who live on the face of the whole earth. Be
alert at all times, praying that you may have the strength
to escape all these things that will take place, and to stand
before the Son of Man.

■ ■ ■

Dissipation. Not one of the words that normally falls of the
tongue during an average day. We are too distracted with a
thousand things to do to be floating such vocabulary. But
that is the nature of dissipation - being scattered, dispersed.
All it takes is one moment, one blink in which we turn our
heads, lose our focus and everything crumbles. Our energies
are scattered with the concerns for others. We cannot take
away their worries but somehow worrying for them seems
like something we can do. In this season of Advent - a time
of waiting and expectation - and the voice of the Lord seems
to be saying, "Hush, little one...I'll be there soon....watch for
me."

■ ■ ■

Come, Lord Jesus, come quickly. Amen.

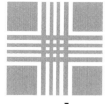

December 18

Mark 1:1-3
In the beginning of the good news of Jesus Christ, the Son of God. As it is written in the prophet Isaiah, "See I am sending my messenger ahead of you, who will prepare your way; the voice of one crying out in the wilderness: 'Prepare the way of the Lord, make his paths straight'"

■ ■ ■

I have this re-occurring dream. It is always a little different, different location, different people. The plot is always the same. There is a tornado coming and I am trying to warn people, but no one is listening. I chalk it up to eating pizza too late at night and watching the Wizard of Oz too much as a child. It does serve me in helping to understand what it might have been like for John as a voice crying in the wilderness. The tornado that John the Baptist proclaimed was certainly one which would stir up everything and change the human landscape forever and not without death and a few scars. The difference with the tornado that is Jesus is that such a wind is truly good news.

■ ■ ■

Lord God, bless the wind with your spirit and may we hear in it the voice of one calling out to us. Amen.

December 19

John 35:35-36
Jesus began to weep. So the Jews said, "See how he loved him!"

■ ■ ■

I asked the question at the beginning of a youth group meeting. "When was the last time you cried and for what reason?" It is a good question. It can give us a clue about what is important to us, but not everyone cries or needs such clues in their lives. Tears can roll because of something or someone for whom we feel passionately. Jesus loved Lazarus. Those who were watching could see it. But Jesus also hated death. The one place in scripture where we see Christ's tears is the place where his two great passions collide - his love for God's people and his hatred of death. As we draw near to Christmas, we are reminded that the Christ child was born to die because God wanted to get rid of tears forever. Perhaps those who don't cry very often are closer to the Kingdom truth than they know.

■ ■ ■

Lord God, bind our wounds, mend our sorrows, dry our tears and get us ready to dance. Amen.

December 20

Isaiah 61:10
I will greatly rejoice in the Lord, my whole being shall exult in my God; for he has clothed me with the garments of salvation, he has covered me with the robe of righteousness, as a bridegroom decks himself with a garland, and as a bride adorns herself with her jewels.

■ ■ ■

The second most annoying moment in my morning is trying to decide what to wear. (For those who need to know, the first is looking in the mirror.) I have pretty basic and rather simple clothing taste, and yet it is still a decision on which I spend too much energy. God is honored when I spend as much, if not more energy, on how I greet people throughout the day, deal with a clerk in a store, or respond to someone with a problem I can help. God gives us our salvation to wear from the inside out for the sake of those in need.

■ ■ ■

Lord God, today let us take your grace off the hanger and wear it with comfort and joy. Amen.

December 21

Psalm 126:1-2
When the LORD restored the fortunes of Zion, we were like
those who dream. Then our mouth was filled with laughter,
and our tongue with shouts of joy; then it was said among
the nations, "The LORD has done great things for them."

■ ■ ■

The people of Israel understood themselves as existing as a
nation, a whole people, even when they had no home, even
when their temple was destroyed, even when they were
scattered by their enemies. The Body of Christ which is the
Church visible in our midst is more whole when we see
ourselves as living parts of each other. We are whole when
we are leaning on one another in times of profound struggle
and rejoicing when there is cause for joy. We can rejoice
together with one another over the great things the Lord
has done for us - even over the sublime joy of being God's
children safe and asleep and dreaming.

■ ■ ■

Guide us waking, Lord and guard us sleeping that we may
rejoice in the great things you have done for us. Amen.

December 22

Luke 1: 30-32
The angel said to her, "Do not be afraid, Mary, for you have found favor with God. And now, you will conceive in your womb and bear a son, and you will name him Jesus. He will be great, and will be called the Son of the most high

■ ■ ■

Okay, so Mary (1) has an angel talking to her; (2) Is told she will have a baby; (3) it's boy; (4) Here's his name; (5) He's gonna be great; (6) his kingdom will be Gi-normous and last forever. Mary, despite her youth, is a practical woman - she says, "Let's go back to Point #2." None of those wonderful promises will ever happen without God doing the impossible. The angel doesn't answer her question but says that impossible stuff doesn't stand in the way of God's plans. Our plans are thwarted by closed doors, minds, and hearts all the time. Sometimes we find another way, but often we can only treat our wounds and grieve. Faith in what seems impossible is a leap for everyone. It was for Mary and it is for all of us. It helps when we take in the whole picture - a God with a plan to save his people.

■ ■ ■

Help us to believe in the impossible and to have faith in your plans, Lord. Amen.

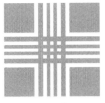

December 23

John 1:22
Then they said to him, "Who are you? Let us have an
answer for those who sent us. What do you say about
yourself?"

■ ■ ■

I was asked to perform a wedding for young couple. I knew the woman well but I did not know her fiancé. The woman was beautiful, brilliant and gifted in many ways. I started my conversation abruptly asking him "Who are you?" The tone of my voice gave away my protectiveness. He knew I wanted to hear that he was someone remarkable enough to be matched with her. He looked at me for a long time, trying to think of something wonderful that he could say about himself to convince me that he was an equally awesome person. He started a thought and then stopped. Finally he looked at me and said, "I'm just a guy." I immediately liked him for his sense of humility and I immediately apologized for my blunt inquisition. John the Baptist was originally thought to be someone greater than he was. He could have claimed some glory for himself but he didn't. When asked, "Who are you?" He knew he was "just a guy" and defined himself in terms of his mission - a voice crying in the wilderness to prepare for the Lord.

■ ■ ■

Lord God, we are your children - members of the royal family - may we claim our identity by being your servants. Amen.

December 24

Micah 5:2
But you, O Bethlehem of Ephrathah, who are one of the
little clans of Judah, from you shall come forth for me one
who is to rule in Israel, whose origin is from of old, from
ancient days.

■ ■ ■

Any place I have ever lived, there has always been a little
town nearby that became the butt of people's jokes. When I
lived in Nashville, the people liked to pick on the name of
the town of Bucksnort. In Texas, Snook was the town name
that was synonymous for a little town noteworthy for its
funny name. Travelers would even stop on the road to take
pictures by the road sign. Sometimes the joking had to do
with a funny sounding name or a town's lack of progress.
The prophet Micah speaking hundreds of years before Jesus
birth must have evoke smirks and laughter at the idea of
the Messiah born in Bethlehem, a Bucksnort-like town.
Indeed, Jesus was born in such a town and his humble birth
elevated every small town in the world. At his coming,
Jesus elevated us all no matter who or where we are.

■ ■ ■

Prepare in us room for your birth again and again so that
we may in humility become the manger for your grace.
Amen.

December 25

Matthew 21:9-11
The crowds that went ahead of him and that followed were
shouting, "Hosanna to the Son of David! Blessed is the one
who comes in the name of the Lord! Hosanna in the highest
heaven!" When he entered Jerusalem, the whole city was in
turmoil, asking, "Who is this?" The crowds were saying,
"This is the prophet Jesus from Nazareth in Galilee."

■　■　■

Leaders come and go. We have read the histories of those
who have their moments in the sun. This Jesus, however,
lingers on lips of followers still. Still his name is shouted
and even now there are those of us who watch the drama
and ask the ancient question: "Who is this?" Even more we
want to know "Who is this person to me?" To enter truly
into the Christmas story is to ask that question. God asked
the same question when looking at us. "Who is this person
to me?" His response was to send his only Son to us and for
us. Christmas is God's answer to the question of who we are
to him. God answered, "Everything."

■　■　■

Through the coming of your son, Lord, may we make room
for the Christ child, our Savior. Amen.

December 26

Psalm 16: 10-11
For you will not abandon me to the grave, nor let your holy one see the pit. You will show me the path of life; in your presence there is fullness of joy, and in your right hand are pleasures forevermore.

■ ■ ■

There is a John Denver song about an uncle "name of Matthew." The song told the story of a twister that killed Matthew's family and destroyed his home and how this uncle came to live with them. He brought with him only his family Bible and his faith "solid as a stone." The refrain of the song said, "Joy was just a thing he was raised on..." What a gift it is that we can give our children to raise them with joy. Life does have its pits and graves, but always there is joy. There is joy enough for everyone. There is joy enough to be raised on. There is the fullness of joy in the presence of the Lord.

■ ■ ■

Holy God, thank you for raising us up with joy. Amen.

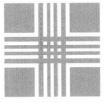

December 27

Romans 16:25-27
Now to God who is able to strengthen you according to my
gospel and the proclamation of Jesus Christ, according to
the revelation of the mystery that was kept secret for long
ages but is now disclosed, and through the prophetic
writings is made known to all the Gentiles, according to the
command of the eternal God, to bring about the obedience of
faith - to the only wise God, through Jesus Christ, to whom
be the glory forever! Amen.

■ ■ ■

In the news recently, I saw a picture of a coin that was over
1000 years old, found near the Sea of Galilee. It bears the
words "Jesus the King of messiahs." With each new
archeological find, new pieces of our ancient past are
revealed. Some of the pieces bear witness to what we
already have learned, some pieces contradict long-held
theories and some create mystery. What we have needed to
know to be God's faithful people has been made known to us
through the scriptures and the testimonies of lives changed.
God became flesh and dwelt among us and has been
revealing himself to us in the stories of his disciples, in the
bread and wine of communion, in the water of our baptisms,
in the grace that is unearthed for us every day.

■ ■ ■

Help us to unearth the radiance of your love and grace,
Lord. Amen.

December 28

I Thessalonians 5:19-21
Do not quench the Spirit. Do not despise the words of prophets, but test everything; hold fast to what is good

■ ■ ■

I went to a workshop during which the leader wore a t-shirt with a buttoned-down sweater. Our group could see that the t-shirt had bold letters that said "ALWAYS QUESTION AUTHORITY." Since he was obviously the local authority on the issue we were discussing, we took it as a challenge to bombard him with questions through the morning. In the afternoon, the leader ceremoniously removed his sweater and turned to prepare notes on the flip chart. The back of his t-shirt read, "WHEN AUTHORITY SPEAKS, LISTEN!" There is nothing wrong with questioning God, God's Word, or God's messengers. It is when we throw the baby out with the bathwater that gets us into trouble. When the baby we are throwing out is the Christ child, we are truly fools.

■ ■ ■

With every breath, Lord, make us grateful to be alive in your grace. Amen.

December 29

Hebrews 10:10
And it is by God's will that we have been sanctified through
the offering of the body of Jesus Christ once for all.

■ ■ ■

What a strange season Christmas is. It is dazzling in its brightness and genuine good spirit. It is exhausting in the demands it makes both in time and finances on families. It is the great news of God's coming into the world. It is the reminder that the baby born in Bethlehem so meek and mild was born to die. God chose to send his Son into the world. We chose to kill him. God chose to let his death become our death so that we might have life in him. Woven into the dancing Christmas lights and the holiday cheer is the painful story of our humanity. The hope for us all is in a child born in humility and was acquainted with suffering and humiliation and a brutal and unjust death. There is joy in Christmas not because of wrapping paper and egg nog. There is joy because God willed it to be.

■ ■ ■

Holy God, your will is more powerful than any of the obstacles of our human sin. Help us kneel more quickly. Amen.

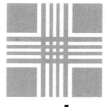

December 30

Isaiah 52:7-10
How beautiful upon the mountains are the feet of the
messenger who announces peace, who brings good news,
who announces salvation, who says to Zion, "Your God
reigns."...... The Lord has bared his holy arm before the eyes
of all the nations; and all the ends of the earth shall see the
salvation of our God.

■ ■ ■

Feet of the messenger and holy arms. Arms and feet. Such
basic, human parts. One of the first adventures of discovery
in our infancy is finding our own hands and feet. We
discover that they are attached to us and that we can
control them. The incredible part of the story of Christmas
is that at one point in his life, Jesus Christ - the Son of the
Living God - was doing nothing more and nothing less than
discovering his own hands and feet. And oh, what he did
with those hands and feet.

■ ■ ■

May our feet bring good news and may our arms bear one
another's burdens in this season of the Christ Child. Amen.

December 31

Psalm 89:1-2
I will sing of your steadfast love, O LORD, forever; with my
mouth I will proclaim your faithfulness to all generations. I
declare that your steadfast love is established forever; your
faithfulness is as firm as the heavens.

■　■　■

I have walked through enough ordinary days that I know
how quickly the easy path changes to a stiff climb or falls
away completely into a pit of shifting sand. A phone call, a
letter, the tone of a voice, words unsaid can turn a road to
mud. It only takes a couple of distracted turns in the forest
of "too many things to do" before we are quite lost in a
blizzard of our own making. One truth remains. One light
shines. We are loved by the Creator of the Universe. No
matter the strength of the enemy that bears down on us
and no matter the missteps we make ourselves along the
way - Christ entered our ordinary days and never has and
never will leave us unloved or alone. He is with us as this
year ends and forever more.

■　■　■

For all, Lord, who feel unloved, alone, afraid, confused,
make your love known and it would be our privilege to be
used for your purposes. Amen.

About the Author

Deb Grant was born in Springfield, Massachusetts and lived with her family in Agawam, Massachusetts until leaving for college. She attended Barrington College which was located in Rhode Island at the time. The college has since merged with Gordon College. She graduated from Barrington in 1975 with an under-graduate degree in English and Biblical Studies. Grant started seminary at Gordon-Conwell Theological Seminary in Massachusetts and transferred to Trinity Lutheran Seminary in Columbus, Ohio where she earned her Masters of Divinity degree in 1981.

Grant was ordained as a pastor in the American Lutheran Church (now ELCA) on September 6, 1981. Since then, she has served congregations in Tennessee, South Carolina and Texas. Her ministry career includes being the Lutheran campus pastor at Texas A&M University.

Grant's other publications include her first book, *Pedestrian Theology, the first volume of ELOGOS* and *The Jesse Tree* (Creative Communications for the Parish). She is also a frequent contributor to the devotional periodicals *Christ in our Home* and *Word in Season* (Augsburg Fortress).

Deb Grant continues to write ELOGOS as a daily email devotional to which anyone may subscribe. To subscribe to ELOGOS emails go to:
www.elogosdailydevotions.com.
Deb Grant can be contacted by email:
revdeb@jazzwater.com

Other Works by Deb Grant

Pedestrian Theology
Discovering Faith One Step At a Time
Langmarc Publishing, 2005
Amazon.com

What readers are saying:

"Deb Grant offers her story—at once filled with humor and pathos, sin and sanctification—as a gift to all of us "pedestrians" who are trying to make sense of our own walks through life. The book tells the truth in a style that echoes Frederick Buechner and Walter Wangerin, Jr. It is a book for everyone who has suffered loss, faced their demons, and reached for God and for all who want to assist others in doing the same."
—*Dr. Brad A. Binau, Associate Professor of Pastoral Theology at Trinity Lutheran Seminary, Columbus, Ohio*

"Whether you are a doubter searching for assurance or a believer craving insight, Pedestrian Theology delivers a unique road map to a faithful life. Through wit, artistry, and raw introspection, Deb Grant reveals what it means to be found by God, saved by the cross, and liberated by love. This exploration of original sin, forgiveness, and faith is a picture of a life grounded in grace."
—*Erika Abel, Research Fellow, University of Texas MD Anderson Cancer Center, Smithville, Texas*

ELOGOS
Daily Devotions for Down to Earth Disciples
Winner – USA Best Books Awards
Prayer and Devotionals
Finalist – NIEA Book Awards
Spirituality